The Order in Which We Do Things
The Poetry of Tom Wayman

The Order in Which We Do Things
The Poetry of Tom Wayman

Selected
with an
introduction by
Owen Percy
and an
afterword by
Tom Wayman

Wilfrid Laurier University Press acknowledges the support of the Canada Council for the Arts for our publishing program. We acknowledge the financial support of the Government of Canada through the Canada Book Fund for our publishing activities.

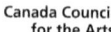 

Library and Archives Canada Cataloguing in Publication

Wayman, Tom, 1945–
[Poems. Selections]
    The order in which we do things : the poetry of Tom Wayman / selected by Owen Percy ; with an introduction by Owen Percy and an afterword by Tom Wayman.

(Laurier Poetry series)
Includes bibliographical references.
Issued in print and electronic formats.
ISBN 978-1-55458-995-1 (pbk.).—ISBN 978-1-55458-997-5 (epub).—ISBN 978-1-55458-996-8 (pdf)

    I. Percy, Owen, writer of introduction, editor of compilation II. Title. III. Title: Poetry of Tom Wayman. IV. Series: Laurier poetry series

PS8595.A9A6 2014   C811'.54   C2013-907640-9   C2013-907641-7

© 2014 Wilfrid Laurier University Press
Waterloo, Ontario N2L 3C5, Canada
www.wlupress.wlu.ca

Cover photograph by Rod Currie. Cover design and text design by P.J. Woodland.

Every reasonable effort has been made to acquire permission for copyright material used in this text, and to acknowledge all such indebtedness accurately. Any errors and omissions called to the publisher's attention will be corrected in future printings.

No part of this publication may be reproduced, stored in a retrieval system or transmitted, in any form or by any means, without the prior written consent of the publisher or a licence from The Canadian Copyright Licensing Agency (Access Copyright). For an Access Copyright licence, visit www.accesscopyright.ca or call toll free to 1-800-893-5777.

Table of Contents

Foreword, *Neil Besner* / vii
Biographical Note / viii
Introduction: Wayman in Print: "He Do the *Polis* in Different Voices,"
    Owen Percy / xi

Days: Construction / 1
Picketing Supermarkets / 2
Wayman in Love / 3
The Country of Everyday: Literary Criticism / 4
The Factory Hour / 6
The Old Power / 8
Industrial Music / 10
Factory Time / 12
Garrison / 15
Friday Night in Early September at Morris and Sara Wayman's Farm,
    Roseneath, Ontario / 21
White Hand / 23
Silos / 25
Paper, Scissors, Stone / 27
The Face of Jack Munro / 29
A Cursing Poem: This Poem Wants Gordon Shrum to Die / 43
The Poet / 46
Defective Parts of Speech: Official Errata / 47
Did I Miss Anything? / 48
The Man Who Logged the West Ridge / 49
For William Stafford (1914–1993) / 51
War on a Round Planet / 53

Cup / 55

Epithalamium for a Former Lover / 56

Calgary / 59

Postmodern 911 / 61

Mt. Gimli Pashtun / 64

Air Support / 68

Whistle / 70

The White Dogs / 73

Minutes / 75

Breath / 77

Afterword: Work and Silence, *Tom Wayman* / 79

Acknowledgements / 87

Foreword

Early in the twenty-first century, poetry in Canada—writing and publishing it, reading and thinking about it—finds itself in a strangely conflicted place. We have many strong poets continuing to produce exciting new work, and there is still a small audience for poetry; but increasingly, poetry is becoming a vulnerable art, for reasons that don't need to be rehearsed.

But there are things to be done: we need more real engagement with our poets. There needs to be more access to their work in more venues—in classrooms, in the public arena, in the media—and there need to be more, and more different kinds, of publications that make the wide range of our contemporary poetry more widely available.

The hope that animates this series from Wilfrid Laurier University Press is that these volumes help to create and sustain the larger readership that contemporary Canadian poetry so richly deserves. Like our fiction writers, our poets are much celebrated abroad; they should just as properly be better known at home.

Our idea is to ask a critic (sometimes himself a poet) to select thirty-five poems from across a poet's career; write an engaging, accessible introduction; and have the poet himself write an afterword. In this way, we think that the usual practice of teaching a poet through eight or twelve poems from an anthology is much improved upon; and readers in and out of classrooms will have more useful, engaging, and comprehensive introductions to a poet's work. Readers might also come to see more readily, we hope, the connections among, as well as the distances between, the life and the work.

It was the ending of an Al Purdy poem that gave Margaret Laurence the epigraph for *The Diviners*: "but they had their being once / and left a place to stand on." Our poets still do, and they are leaving many places to stand on. We hope that this series helps, variously, to show how and why this is so.

—*Neil Besner*
General Editor

Biographical Note

Thomas Ethan Wayman was born in Hawkesbury, Ontario, in 1945. His father, a chemist in the pulp industry, moved the family to Prince Rupert on the coast of northern British Columbia when Wayman was seven. In 1959 the family relocated to Vancouver—the city that would help to shape Wayman's social consciousness and would become the scene of much of his activism and the backdrop to many of his poems. After discovering the California Beat poets in high school, Wayman began his B.A. in English at the University of British Columbia, where he studied with Earle Birney and Dorothy Livesay (who supervised his Honours thesis). He simultaneously worked as a reporter for the *Vancouver Sun* and was editor-in-chief of the UBC student newspaper, *The Ubyssey*, in 1965–66. He graduated in 1966 and moved to southern California to pursue graduate studies at the University of California at Irvine, where he earned his M.F.A. in English and Creative Writing. He taught for a year in Fort Collins, Colorado, before returning to Vancouver in 1969 to join the industrial workforce as a construction and demolition labourer, factory assemblyman, and high school English marker.

Wayman's experiences in the classroom, on the road, and on the job came to temper and hone his literary voice, and they became the inspiration for his first book of poems, *Waiting for Wayman*, published to critical acclaim in Canada in 1973. Since then, he has gone on to publish nineteen books of poetry, three works of prose fiction, three collections of essays on labour arts (as well as several uncollected articles and essays), and to edit six poetry anthologies, many on the theme of daily employment. Wayman has been equally active in his struggle for workers' rights and education in BC; he co-founded the Vancouver Industrial Writers' Union (1979–96) and the Vancouver Centre of the Kootenay School of Writing (1984–87) and was founding president of the Faculty and Staff union at Nelson's Kootenay School of the Arts. In addition to serving as writer-in-residence at Simon Fraser University and the Universities of Windsor, Alberta, Winnipeg, and Toronto, Wayman has been on faculty at Colorado State University, Wayne State University, the Banff School of Fine Arts, David Thompson University Centre, Kwantlen College, the Kootenay School of Writing, Okanagan University College, the Kootenay School of the Arts, the Victoria School of Writing, Douglas College, and the University of Calgary, from which he retired in 2010. He also held a Fulbright Visiting Chair in Creative Writing at

Arizona State University and the Ralph Gustafson Chair of Poetry at Malaspina University-College, both in 2007.

Wayman has honed his renowned public voice and persona in factory lunchrooms and on picket lines, in union halls and contract negotiation sessions, as well as in classrooms and onstage. Celebrated for his entertaining and poignant public readings, he has been awarded the A.J.M. Smith Prize, *Poetry Northwest's* Helen Bullis Prize, first prize in the 1976 US National Bicentennial Poetry Awards, the Acorn-Plantos Award for People's Poetry, and the Canadian Authors Association medal for poetry. He has been shortlisted for the Governor General's Award and B.C.'s Dorothy Livesay Poetry Prize. Since 1989, he has been the Squire of Appledore, the acreage on Perry Ridge in the Selkirk Mountains near Winlaw, B.C., where he makes his home. He spends his time reading, writing, growing vegetables, fending off deer, cross-country skiing, rewriting, hiking, canoeing, rewriting again, serving on various local arts boards as well as that of the Calgary International Spoken Word Festival, and generally failing spectacularly at being retired.

Introduction

Wayman in Print: "He Do the *Polis* in Different Voices"

> See! Without labour nothing prospers well!
> — Sophocles, *Electra* (945)

> Meet me at the bottom, don't lag behind
> Bring me my boots and shoes
> You can hang back or fight your best on the front line
> Sing a little bit of these workingman's blues.
> — Bob Dylan, "Workingman's Blues #2"

The Order in Which We Do Things marks more than forty years in print for Tom Wayman. To say that he has been prolific in those years would be an understatement; in his nineteen books of poetry since 1973—nearly 800 poems on more than 2000 pages—Wayman has developed one of the most recognizable voices and personas in Canadian poetry. The poems presented here are broadly representative of Wayman's larger oeuvre. We hope that, in addition to introducing new readers to the world of Wayman and reminding the initiated of the range and prescience of his finest work, *The Order in Which We Do Things* might serve as a springboard from which all can dive into the larger pool of verse—whatever works for them—from which these poems are drawn.

    Like Walt Whitman, another public poetic persona, Wayman contains multitudes; his poems speak to and from a wide range of perspectives, exploring the universals of work, love, sex, death, and much else besides. One minute Wayman is conceptualizing string theory, the next he is contemplating the politics of taking a shit on company time; he is lamenting the banality of grading student essays and then raging against Canada's participation in the war in Afghanistan. And inasmuch as it is always a version of Wayman at the helm of a poem, it is always also what Wendy Keitner identifies as "a contemporary Everyman" (par. 2)—someone who speaks his own truth, but in whose truth we see a version of our own, of our friends' and family's, and of that of the larger *polis*—that is, of the communities and collectives to which we belong in relation to the forces of industry, authority, and capital that would have us believe, terrifyingly, that we are alone, powerless, and at their mercy. As R. Alexander Kizuk puts it, in Wayman, "the exploded self converts to a kind of figural labour in which the poet-penseroso becomes his own errant Tribe and Glory" (par. 26); in a Wayman poem, the voice *is* the collective—the construed universal within the specific.

But inasmuch as Wayman is never *just* Wayman, Wayman is always Wayman; like Whitman, Al Purdy, or Leonard Cohen, he is often a distinct persona within his own verse and the central, guiding referent to the real world and the everyday lived experience the majority of his poems revolve around. So Wayman's "Wayman" is not Wayman himself but, like all narrative personas, a performative, universalized amplification of certain aspects of the poet's self. The persona is, like us, by turns angry and passive, loving and loathing, self-conscious and self-righteous, learned and learning. Wayman's is a voice that speaks as authentically as it can, and that aspires, as he himself put it in his 1983 collection of essays, *Inside Job*, "to share with other people what I noticed about the condition of being alive" (9) in the hope that they might recognize and celebrate some solidarity in the shared human experience.

As a poet, Wayman recognizes and celebrates this solidarity in the real-life voices of others, too. While he might seem to have little in common with a notoriously cryptic poet like T.S. Eliot, Wayman in fact shares the great anglophile's penchant for finding the poetry inherent in the real-life language of people, as Eliot does in *The Waste Land*. Wayman's world is a sight more hopeful than Eliot's, but the poets share a suspicion of and disillusionment with the failures of institutionality and modern capitalist material culture. While not quite the heap of broken images of Eliot's post-WWI moment, Wayman's portrait of industrialized society today is one that relies on the similar tactic of harnessing voices, real or approximate, from across the social spectrum and allowing them to speak in their own idioms alongside one another. The result is rarely as disjointed and apocalyptic as it is in Eliot, but the approach achieves a similar collective murmur from which singular voices can emerge and retreat. Consider in the coming pages, for example, the traumatized conversation among a group of workers who witness an industrial accident in "The Country of Everyday: Literary Criticism," or "Garrison," wherein the titular subject explores his vanities and frustrations, and ends up telling the story of an entire generation running from a social order into which they do not comfortably fit, toward a hopeful future to which they never manage to catch up.

Wayman is known primarily as a work writer, and thus his craft is *poïesis* (from the Ancient Greek "to make")—making things happen, making a change, making a difference, making a ruckus, making the most of our time.

As a manual labourer, union organizer, teacher, and mentor, he has done and been proximate to the labour of many, and he has never lived, even as a poet, apart from the society that builds, maintains, and upholds the order in which we do things. As a result, his poems proffer an honest and candid consideration of the ideological underpinnings, practical realities, and subtle beauties of a life lived on job sites and picket lines, in union halls, classrooms, and book-stuffed offices, and on the page itself. Put simply, Wayman believes that "[w]e live in a society that hides from itself the basis of its existence" ("Visible Consequences" xv) because its art has actively refused to acknowledge the role, value, and vagaries that work plays in the day-to-day lives of its citizens. As he discusses in the Afterword to this collection, most of Wayman's poetic and non-fictional writing since the 1960s aims to respond to the dearth of artistic representation of the activity with which most of us are centrally preoccupied during the waking hours of our lives, and to correct the portrait of life in Canada drawn by most of its literature of a country in which nobody seems to work. It remains Wayman's contention that "if we are to consider how to alter the world for the better, we surely must start from an unflinchingly honest portrayal of how the world is now" ("Afterword: Work, Money, Authenticity" 125), and this includes, of course, depictions of daily work, as in poems like "Days: Construction" and "The Factory Hour"; considerations of what it means and costs to work, as in "Defective Parts of Speech: Official Errata" and "White Hand"; and the stark recognition that all work is not valued or remunerated equally or fairly, as in "The Old Power" and "Paper, Scissors, Stone."

What is most notable about Wayman's work poems in this respect is not that they are the first or only poems to depict work in Canada but that they are among the first to fall into the category Wayman calls the new work writing, characterized by being written "by an insider speaking about her or his own workplace experiences rather than by an outsider" (*A Country* 150). Historically, on the rare occasions when literature has described work at all, it has been the province of outsiders—non-workers at the jobs they describe— who tend toward romanticization and omission in their depictions of labour. The new work writing assumes one of the basic tenets of Marxist philosophy: that "the ruling ideas of any age are the ideas of its ruling class" (Wayman, *Inside Job* 38), and that it remains in the best interest of said class to minimize the depiction and discussion of work in art in favour of shinier, happier, sexier things that might placate us into distraction from the realities of our working lives. Instead, and in order to combat what he calls the "purposeful confusion generated on behalf of corporations and governments with a vested interest in having people turn away from understanding their own daily lives" (*Songs* 9),

Wayman adopts the term "Internal Realism"— "art that is us showing ourselves to ourselves" (*Inside Job* 48). As such, what he considers new in his poems "is not experiments in poetic form but in content ... [but] the pervasive consciousness that the conditions of daily work in our time is what shapes the world ... this poetry also rejects the concept of art as a means of escape from the everyday" ("Afterword: Work, Money, Authenticity" 124). So what is new in the new work writing is in fact what is old—the fact *that* we work—expressed culturally, as the beginning of a mature conversation about our role, value, experience, and power within, well, the existing orders in which we do things.

In this light, Wayman does not see poetry as an end in and of itself, but as "a tool useful for beneficial social ends" (qtd. in Guichon 43). Paradoxically, poetry remains the ideal vehicle for this kind of change precisely because of its relative unpopularity. In 1979 Wayman put forth the suggestion that "[i]n an age when every form of communication seems encouraged to tell lies by the hope of making money, only private speech and poetry are left to present the truth" ("Afterword: *A Planet Mostly Sea*" 65). In *Songs Without Price*, a lecture he gave as the 2007 Ralph Gustafson Chair in Poetry at Malaspina University-College, Wayman explained that "[p]oetry's great opportunity to express important concepts ... occurs because the art form exists in the shadowlands outside the money economy ... poetry is both literally and metaphorically priceless" (9). That is, poetry is wrought from what we might call unalienated labour (work in which the worker's interests are not subsumed or determined by those of an employer or overseer), because it is not popular enough to garner the interests and investments of the powers that be (always ultimately for their own profit), and thus it remains a form of social communication, comparatively unbesmirched by the interests of the market economy, wherein conscious radical alterity can be expressed and celebrated.

The poems selected here are presented in the approximate order in which Wayman has done things since he began to publish in the late 1960s; they begin where Wayman began, on the construction sites and in the factories of industrial Vancouver where he made his living during the day (and which he wrote about at night), and they end in the relative present, with poems from his 2013 book *Winter's Skin*. Some of the poems included, like "The Face of Jack Munro" and even "Mt. Gimli Pashtun," are no longer the urgent, pulled-from-the-headlines anthems about the BC public sector strike (1983) and Canada's combat role in the most recent war in Afghanistan (2001–2011) that they were at their first utterance. Instead, they survive as something like what is now called literary journalism, offering a creative window into the universal struggles at the heart of specific events and moments. Wayman, though, remains more than just an anthropologist of the working Canadian citizenry, because in poems like these the spirit of the human struggle can be heard in and among a sea of voices—the same spirit of resistance against tyranny and political oppression, against sexism and racism and classism that has given rise most recently to the Arab Spring in the Middle East and to the Occupy and Idle No More movements that erupted in North America and Europe in the face of rising corporate and government malfeasance, increasingly faceless institutionality in the workforce, and ruthless, reckless industrialization and militarization. The spirit of emancipation and democracy does not age.

Indeed, the great sad irony is that many of Wayman's activist poems written in and for their specific moments up to four decades ago remain fresh and poignant today, not only because of the energy and spirit of the language but because the social ideals to which they aspire—justice, democracy, community, equality—remain largely unattained. In fact, some poems have proven to be downright prescient in their specifics *and* their universals; it seems impossible that 1973's "Picketing Supermarkets," for example, could have been written before Michael Pollan's *The Omnivore's Dilemma* (2006) or Alisa Smith and J.B. MacKinnon's *The 100-Mile Diet* (2007). But it was. Likewise, Wayman's updating of Eliot's *The Waste Land*, "Asphalt Hours, Asphalt Air" (from 1979's *A Planet Mostly Sea*) is set against the crumbling backdrop of Detroit, a once-beloved metropolis whose infrastructure and spirit have been bankrupted in all but name. The poem, too long to include here in its entirety and too eerily coherent to excerpt justly, could have never predicted that the very corporate interests that once made the city great, employed and sustained millions of North Americans, would *again* ransack it and leave it for dead. But it did. In this sense, Wayman's poetry often bears witness to our collective unwillingness or inability to break out of the boom-and-bust order in which we continue to do things.

In terms of style, Wayman speaks plainly. His conversational, often prosaic idiom is neither accidental nor arbitrary; it is, clearly, a style lovingly developed out of his close reading of socially active Beat poets like Lew Welch and Kenneth Rexroth and of his late mentor and friend, Al Purdy. In his elegy upon Purdy's death Wayman pays his dues:

> His gift to me
> was his rambling: his itinerant lines and
> peripatetic stanzas—apparently relaxed, inquisitive, opinionated,
> exactly like someone talking:
>
> a conversation with the reader so cunningly shaped
> that the choice of structure or other artistic details
> is not the point of the piece, any more than a news story
> reveals its architecture. ("In Memory of A.W. Purdy" 85–92)

While the conversational "shape" of Wayman's poems may not seem the point, it does achieve the clear effect of engaging any and all readers who might come across it in spite of themselves. This sentiment is, of course, the same one that led William Wordsworth and Samuel Taylor Coleridge to break so thunderously with tradition in their poems, revisions, and prefaces to *Lyrical Ballads* in the book's 1798, 1800, and 1802 editions. They famously aspired to embody the "real language of men in a state of vivid sensation" (287) and "to make the incidents of common life interesting by tracing in them, truly though not ostentatiously, the primary laws of our nature" (289–90) in hopes that "a class of poetry would be produced, well adapted to interest mankind permanently, and not unimportant in the multiplicity and in the quality of its moral relations" (287–88). These remain Wayman's hopes, borne across the decades by the consistent plainspokenness of the everyday that infiltrates a genre widely assumed to traffic in an exclusive, elite vocabulary.

Wayman has always been an oral poet. His third book, 1975's *Money and Rain: Tom Wayman Live!*, was sold with a cassette tape of him reading his poems, while the text itself contains prose preambles and introductions that emulate the experience of being at a reading. This technique, which he revisits in 2012's *Dirty Snow*, underscores the debt owed by Canada's Spoken Word scene to poets like Wayman whose bread and butter is in firing up an audience, a picket line, or a classroom. He is, in many ways, more of a polemic folksinger on a stage than a poet on a page, and much of his verse has more in common with protest songs (Utah Phillips's "Bread and Roses," Woody Guthrie's "Union Burying Ground," Bob Dylan's "Maggie's Farm," and Ani DiFranco's "Your Next Bold Move" come to mind) than it might with a collection of sonnets or ghazals. Wayman is, in this sense, a unique hybrid of a writer—something like the Springsteen of the Slocan—paying heed to workers married to a factory that takes their hearing but gives them some semblance of a life. But like all great folk- and protest singers, Wayman is frank in his depictions but remains unbowed in his optimism that change is going to come; he is too, then, the Seeger of the Selkirks, humming "We Shall Overcome" and believing, through toil, consciousness, and community, that "we are forever about to succeed" (Wayman, "Against" 89).

As such, his metaphors are not often subtle, his politics are easily discernible (ask Gordon Shrum or Jack Munro—Wayman names names!), and his voice is direct, unambiguous. But to call Wayman's poems simple would be inaccurate. He clarifies in his introduction to 1993's *Did I Miss Anything?*

> Overall, my intention is that the complexities revealed by my poems should be the complications of our everyday existence, rather than newly-created difficulties or mysteries generated by tricks of language or

poetic form. Clarity, honesty, accuracy of statement have been my goals—subject to, naturally, the limits of human discourse found in *every* genre or means of communication … I mean these poems to be a gift; I want my poetry to be a tender, humorous, enraged, piercing, but always accurate depiction of where we are—as individuals functioning in a society, and as members of a rawly self-conscious species now occupying the third planet from a nondescript star. ("Glad I Was Born" 12)

While this description is clearly apt in describing the majority of Wayman's verse, it does not account for the stark, skeletal imagism and haiku sensibility of much of his elegiac and nature poetry (see "Breath," for example), nor does it overtly acknowledge the clear familiarity with and affection for the diverse historical canon of poetry in English that trickles into his practice. Whether he is parodically revamping the epithalamium—a Classical celebratory wedding poem last popular in the early Renaissance—or recasting the aboriginal cursing poem, Wayman's facility with form is always matched by the virulence and authenticity of his language (see "Epithalamium for a Former Lover" and "A Cursing Poem: This Poem Wants Gordon Shrum to Die"). The section "Lost and Found" from 1989's *In a Small House on the Outskirts of Heaven* even comprises found poetry (see "The Poet"), while the pieces from his most recent book (including "Minutes" and "The White Dogs") pay tribute to what he calls his "conceptually oriented colleagues" ("Author's Note" 9) in that the poems riff on literal and figurative cues found in Chilean poet Pablo Neruda's posthumous 1974 collection *Jardín de invierno*.

Despite his considerable public following, academic critics have paid less attention to Wayman than they have to several of his more esoteric and abstract contemporaries, and they have been largely unwilling to consider him as much beyond what Wendy Keitner calls the bardic "heir apparent to Al Purdy and Milton Acorn" (par. 1). He has not yet, for example, been closely read as an ecopoet despite his clear environmental awareness and concern. His writing is steeped in a consciousness of the fragility and resilience, the power and delicacy, the brutality and tenderness of the natural world and what we do in and with it. Consider the prophetically terrifying "Silos" or the nuanced layering of images in "The Man Who Logged the West Ridge," where the man paid to strip the area of its pulp nonetheless "has his home on the Valley floor" (3), and must endure the abuse of his neighbours for the work he does. The poem witnesses "the fir and larch and pine / of the Ridge, its deer and coyote, / snails and hummingbirds" becoming "dollars for a brief time" before being turned into paper and "gone from our Valley" (10–14). To the extent that we are united by the circumstances and the social order in which we live, we are united by the places we find ourselves living, using, and using up.

What Wayman teaches, then, is what you already know—that you are alive, right now; that you are part of a sociopolitical system that might not respect your inherent humanity; but that you are not alone in your experience of the world. The 2007 poem "Invocation" shows how the tasks of the everyday—the labour of toiling to grow something for tomorrow that is better, greener, more nourished and nourishing than it is today—infiltrate everything that we do; the poem is also a clear cry of optimism and hope that Wayman's own verse might share the spirit and the solidarity in which it is written with its readers:

> Poems scribbled, keyed, re-crafted
> and keyed again
> while the sun thrusts in past the marigolds
> at the east window
> as the clock shifts toward
> the irrigation sprinklers' next time to be
> moved, so I return to the desk
> having not only hauled and connected hoses
> over July grass, but en route
> tied a sagging gladiolus stem
> or plucked a few weeds among radish leaves
> causing both soil and moisture to cling to fingers
> that scurry across plastic lettered buttons:
> may your words, whatever their intent, embrace and contain
> this mountain earth, its sky
> and the circling water, O poems.

The poems growing in and on the following pages here contain the world as Wayman lives it; they pick away at the institutions around which we structure and sustain our lives; the paths, pursuits, and pleasures we seek out and endure through our actions as citizens; the experiences we share as beings on a round, gasping planet. This is the poetry of social integrity, of sweat and anger, of love and anxiety, of learning and teaching, of city and country, and of our universal and specific everydays. The product of Wayman's love and work over the last forty years, and of the love and work of the editors, publishers, distributors, and booksellers involved in getting this book into your hands right now, these poems acknowledge, embrace, and contain all of that which has been, is, and is yet to come in each of our labouring, loving, learning lives. *The Order in Which We Do Things* is up to you now. Work it.

—*Owen Percy*

Works Cited

Dylan, Bob. "Workingman's Blues #2." *Modern Times*. Columbia, 2006. CD.

Guichon, Diane. "Tom Wayman, A Poet Reconsidered: A Conversation." Interview. *The Writer's Chronicle* 41.4 (2009): 40–48.

Keitner, Wendy. "Looking for Owls: The Quest Motif in Tom Wayman's Poetry." *Canadian Poetry* 12 (1983). http://canadianpoetry.org/volumes/vol12/keitner.html.

Kizuk, R. Alexander. "The Rhetoric of Emancipation in Canadian Public Poetry: From Tom MacInnes to Tom Wayman." *Canadian Poetry* 44 (1999). http://www.canadianpoetry.ca/cpjrn/vol44/rhetoric_of_emancipation.htm.

Sophocles. *Electra. Tragedies and Fragments in Two Volumes*. Vol. 1. Trans. E.H. Plumptre. Bath: Pitman & Sons, 1914. 189–243.

Wayman, Tom. *A Country Not Considered: Canada, Culture, Work*. Toronto: Anansi, 1993.

———. "Afterword: *A Planet Mostly Sea*." Winnipeg: Turnstone, 1979. 65.

———. "Afterword: Work, Money, Authenticity." *In a Small House on the Outskirts of Heaven*. Madeira Park, BC: Harbour, 1989. 116–27.

———. "Against the Smiling Bastards." *The New Quarterly* 101 (2007): 76–89.

———. "Author's Note." *Winter's Skin*. Fernie, BC: Oolichan, 2013. 9–10.

———. "Glad I Was Born." Introduction to *Did I Miss Anything? Selected Poems 1973–1993*. Madeira Park, BC: Harbour, 1993. 11–16.

———. "In Memory of A.W. Purdy." *My Father's Cup*. Madeira Park, BC: Harbour, 2002. 79–82.

———. *Inside Job: Essays on the New Work Writing*. Madeira Park, BC: Harbour, 1983.

———. "Invocation." *High Speed Through Shoaling Water*. Madeira Park, BC: Harbour, 2007. 143.

———. *Songs Without Price: The Music of Poetry in a Discordant World*. Nanaimo, BC: Institute for Coastal Research/Kentville, NS: Gaspereau, 2008.

———. "Visible Consequences, Invisible Jobs." Introduction to *Paperwork: An Anthology*. Madeira Park, BC: Harbour, 1991. xv–xx.

Wordsworth, William, and Samuel Taylor Coleridge. Preface. 1800 (with 1802 variants). *Lyrical Ballads*. Ed. R.L. Brett and A.R. Jones. London: Routledge Classics, 2005. 286–314.

Days: Construction

Days when the work does not end.
When the bath at home is like
cleaning another tool of the owner's.
A tool which functions better with the dust gone from its pores.
So that tomorrow the beads of sweat
can break out again along trouser-legs and sleeves.

And then bed. Night. The framing continues
inside the head: hammers pound on
through the resting brain. With each blow
the nails sink in, inch by blasted inch.
Now one bends, breaking the rhythm.
Creaks as it's tugged free. A new spike
is pounded in.

The ears ring with it. In the dark
this is the room where construction is.
Blow by blow, the studding goes up.
The joists are levered into place.
The hammers rise.

Picketing Supermarkets

Because all this food is grown in the store
do not take the leaflet.
Cabbages, broccoli and tomatoes
are raised at night in the aisles.
Milk is brewed in the rear storage areas.
Beef produced in vats in the basement.
Do not take the leaflet.
Peanut butter and soft drinks
are made fresh each morning by store employees.
Our oranges and grapes
are so fine and round
that when held up to the lights they cast no shadow.
Do not take the leaflet.

And should you take one
do not believe it.
This chain of stores has no connection
with anyone growing food someplace else.
How could we have an effect on local farmers?
Do not believe it.

The sound here is Muzak, for your enjoyment.
It is not the sound of children crying.
There *is* a lady offering samples
to mark Canada Cheese Month.
There is no dark-skinned man with black hair beside her
wanting to show you the inside of a coffin.
You would not have to look if there was.
And there are no Nicaraguan heroes
in any way connected with the bananas.

Pay no attention to these people.
The manager is a citizen.
All this food is grown in the store.

Wayman in Love

At last Wayman gets the girl into bed.
He is locked in one of those embraces
so passionate his left arm is asleep
when suddenly he is bumped in the back.
"Excuse me," a voice mutters, thick with German.
Wayman and the girl sit up astounded
as a furry gentleman in boots and a frock coat
climbs in under the covers.

"My name is Doktor Marx," the intruder announces
settling his neck comfortably on the pillow.
"I'm here to consider for you the cost of a kiss."
He pulls out a notepad. "Let's see now,
we have the price of the mattress, this room must be rented,
your time off work, groceries for two,
medical fees in case of accidents…."

"Look," Wayman says,
"couldn't we do this later?"
The philosopher sighs, and continues: "You are affected too, Miss.
If you are not working, you are going to resent
your dependent position. This will influence
I assure you, your most intimate moments…."

"Doctor, please," Wayman says. "All we want
is to be left alone."
But another beard, more nattily dressed,
is also getting into the bed.
There is a shifting and heaving of bodies
as everyone wriggles out room for themselves.
"I want you to meet a friend from Vienna,"
Marx says. "This is Doktor Freud."

The newcomer straightens his glasses,
peers at Wayman and the girl.
"I can see," he begins,
"that you have two problems…."

The Country of Everyday: Literary Criticism

"He was in a hurry," Wood said, "the young foreman
only 26, down on his knees at the base of
the heavy lamppost, impatient to push it back on the block.
He was yelling at the rest of us to give him a hand
and didn't see the top of the pole, as it
swayed over and touched the powerline.

"I was looking right at him. There was a flash
and he just folded over onto his side and
turned black: his ears melted.
There were two holes burned in the pavement
where his knees were. Somebody started giving him
mouth-to-mouth, and I said *forget it. I mean, he's dead*."

And there are poets who can enter in
to the heart of a door, and discover the rat inside us
that must be kept caged in the head because it is perfectly sane.

There are poets who claim to know what it's like
to have a crucifix wedged in the throat
unable to swallow, and how the knot of the stomach
turns into a bowl of fire.

But around and ahead of them
is the housewife endlessly washing
linoleum, sheets, fruit dishes, her hands
and the face of a child. And there is the girl who stands
in the cannery line twelve hours in season
to cut out the tips of the fish.
For the paper they tear out to write on
is pulled from the weeks of working graveyard
and all the weariness of millwork, the fatigue
of keeping it going, the urge to reclaim the body
for the hours not working or sleeping
when the body ends too tired for much but a beer and a laugh.

Beside every dazzling image, each line
desperate to search the unconscious
are the thousand hours someone is spending
watching ordinary television.
For every poet who considers the rhythm
of the word "dark" and the word "darkness"
a crew is balancing high on the grid
of a new warehouse roof, gingerly taking the first load of lumber
hauled thirty feet up to them.

For every hour someone reads critical articles
Swede is drunk in a bar again
describing how he caught his sleeve once in the winch of an oil rig
whirling him round till his ribs broke.
And for every rejection of a manuscript
a young apprentice is riding up on the crane
to work his first day on high steel.
"Left my fingerprints in the metal
when I had to grab a beam to get off," he says.
And Ed Shaw stands looking down into the hold
where a cable sprang loose lifting a pallet
and lashed across the dock, just touching one of the crew
whose body they are starting to bring up from the water.

When the poet goes out for a walk in the dusk
listening to his feet on the concrete, pondering
all the adjectives for rain, he is walking on work
of another kind, and on lives that wear down like cement.
Somewhere a man is saying, "Worked twenty years for the City
but I'm retired now."
Sitting alone in a room, in the poorhouse of a pension
he has never read a modern poem.

The Factory Hour

The sun up through a blue mist
draws its own tide: this is the factory hour.
As I drive east, I pass dozens like myself
waiting on the curb for buses, for company crummies,
for car pools; grey plastic lunch buckets,
safety boots, old clothes. All of us pulled
on the same factory tide.

                        The plant's parking lot
is the dock; the small van of the industrial caterers
has opened at the furthest gate through the fence: coffee, cigarettes,
sandwiches. Walking in through the asphalt yard
we enter the hull of the vessel.

The great hold is readying itself for the voyage. Steam
rises slowly from the acid cleaning tanks
near the small parts conveyor and spray booth.
We pass to the racks of cards; sudden clang of machine shears
but otherwise only the hum of voices, generators, compressors.
Click and thump of the cards at the clock. The slow movement
of those already changed into blue coveralls.

The hooter sounds, and we're cast off. First coughs
and the mutter of the forklift engines.
Then the first rivets shot home in the cab shop's metal line.
Air hoses everywhere connected, beginning to hiss, the whir
of the hood line's drills. The first bolts are tightened:
the ship underway on the water of time.

Howl of the routers: smell of fiberglass dust.
Noise of the suction vacuum, the cutter, the roar
of dollies trundled in for a finished hood. And the PA endlessly calling
for partsmen, for foremen, for chargehands:

Neil Watt to Receiving please, Neil Watt.
Jeff Adamanchuck to Sheet Metal.
Dave Giberson to Gear Shop ... to Parts Desk ... Sub-Assembly.

The hooters marking the half-hours, the breaks,
the ship plunging ahead. The PA sounding
Call 1 for the superintendent; Call 273; Call guardhouse; Call switchboard.
Lunch at sea: sprawled by the hoods in ordinary weather
or outside at the doors to the parts-yard if fine; whine of the fans
and the constant shuttling of the forklifts
show that the ship still steams. Then the hooter
returns us back to the hours of eyebolts,
grilles, wiring headlamps, hoodguides, shaping and
sanding smooth the air-cleaner cutouts. On and on
under the whir of the half-ton crane, rattle of the impact wrench,
grating of new hood shells as they are dragged onto a pallet.

To the last note of the hooter: the boat returned to its City.
A final lineup at the timeclock, and out through the doors
to the dockside parking lot. Late afternoon:
I drive into the tide of homebound traffic, headed west now
still moving into the sun.

The Old Power

The old power is still here: pulling into work one morning
to find the access road to the company parking lot
jammed with men and vehicles, more cars
piling up behind, spilling out onto the main street
and down adjacent lanes, everybody arriving
from different directions to stand together
at the gate of the almost-empty lot
(just a few foremen's cars and the night shift of painters)
where five men from the company's sales and service division
on strike for more than a month now
stand with their picket signs.

Early morning dark, and a cold rain.
Five men with sheets of cardboard looped around their necks
changing feet to keep warm, drinking coffee
from the small white cups somebody brought them:
five men in a line, occasionally talking to someone else
but mostly just standing at the very edge of company property
and then a little space
and then all four hundred of us, mixed in
with our lunchpails and boots and the cars that brought us here.

Like an old myth that suddenly works: a marvelous event in a forest
that happens to you personally so that again
you can believe in what you once had clung to
and then abandoned: five sheepish men
in the rain at the end of a road
hold back our hundreds. And this is something
both of us make: they carrying the symbol out in front of us
and we agreeing. So whatever happens here
is ours.

After half an hour in the drizzle, the sky getting lighter,
not a supervisor or foreman in sight,

some of us wander off to the Lougheed Hotel for coffee.
Then, I drive home. And all the while the five men stand there
like pillars of the old power, an idea made flesh,
an idea that works. So that today, Thursday,
no one has to build a single truck

and we can take all the rest of this day in the rain for ourselves.

Industrial Music
for Michael Millar, Michael Taylor, Gary Walsh

After a hundred years they paused
and they heard
music; other things were on the wind
but they heard a music filling in the continent behind them:
their own music, which grew slowly,
starting at the quietest moments
like a flower, or at prayer, and at
work, and then beginning to be pumped through
cash registers, radios, and finally even leaked in
through small grilles in elevators.

But as fast as the melodies get smoothed
into a dollar, a man stands up in a noisy bar and
begins to sing, and another man joins him and
another, until the air is filled again with music,
human voices. And twenty thousand of us
are put in a single vast room
to hear one famous voice with a song rise through amplifiers
and the songs also come from just Bob Garrison
driving his '55 Willys up the Canyon from Siska
on a rainy Saturday and only me and one other
jammed into his front seat listen.

And I remember in the truck factory Boris Hukaluk drumming
everywhere, standing in Cab Electrical
tapping out the intricate rhythms with his wire stripper
and a screwdriver, but Boris also
knows everything about Folding Hoods after years
working at that before, so he gets assigned back on the days
Hoskins doesn't show. And I asked him there
why he didn't ever become a professional musician and he said
I didn't like the life; too many late nights all the time
so he drums weekends in a cabaret, in the house band
without even a name, and does special jobs at New Year's and

drums through his days and years at the factory
his fingers and pencils falling on the metal. One day
we are up at Test fitting a hood and one of the mechanics
picks up Boris' rhythm and sends it back to him
with his wrenches, as best he can, and Boris
grins and stops what he's doing and gives out
another short riff, and this time
a couple of guys try to match him, and Boris laughs
and taps out another complicated run
and this time maybe half a dozen guys start
clumsily pounding away after his lead. And this makes so much noise
(since somebody is banging on a waste can) that the foreman
comes out of his office to find out what's up
but sees Boris and shakes his head and goes back.

Then it's lunch and someone turns a truck radio on, and the music,
rock now, pours into the echoing Test bays
like the wind when somebody rolls aside one of the huge doors
on a cold wet February morning, the wind
flowing in off the river among the parked tires and motors,
the tool boxes, air hoses and containers of oil,
a wind that carries with it all the sounds of the City at work
this day: grudgingly, but alive, and moving.

Factory Time

The day divides neatly into four parts
marked off by the breaks. The first quarter
is a full two hours, 7:30 to 9:30, but that's okay
in theory, because I'm supposed to be fresh, but in fact
after some evenings it's a long first two hours.
Then, a ten-minute break. Which is good
another way, too: the second quarter
thus has ten minutes knocked off, 9:40 to 11:30
which is only 110 minutes, or
to put it another way, if I look at my watch
and it says 11:10
I can cheer up because if I had still been in the first quarter
and had worked for 90 minutes there would be
30 minutes to go, but now there is only
20. If it had been the first quarter, I could expect
the same feeling at 9 o'clock as here I have
when it is already ten minutes after 11.

Then it's lunch: a stretch, and maybe a little walk around.
And at 12 sharp the endless quarter begins:
a full two afternoon hours. And it's only the start
of the afternoon. Nothing to hope for the whole time.
Come to think of it, today
is probably only Tuesday. Or worse, Monday,
with the week barely begun and the day
only just half over, four hours down
and 36 to go this week
(if the foreman doesn't come padding by about 3
some afternoon and ask us all to work overtime).

Now while I'm trying to get through this early Tuesday afternoon
maybe this is a good place to say
Wednesday, Thursday and Friday have their personalities too.
As a matter of fact, Wednesday after lunch

I could be almost happy
because when that 12 noon hooter blast goes
the week is precisely and officially half over.
All downhill from here: Thursday, as you know
is the day before Friday
which means a little celebrating Thursday night
—perhaps a few rounds in the pub after supper—
won't do me any harm. If I don't get much sleep
Thursday night, so what? I can sleep in Saturday.
And Friday right after lunch Mike the foreman appears
with the long cheques dripping out of his hands
and he is so polite to each of us as he passes them over
just like they taught him in foreman school.
After that, not too much gets done.
People go away into a corner and add and subtract like crazy
trying to catch the Company in a mistake
or figuring out what incredible percentage the government
has taken this week, or what the money will actually mean
in terms of savings or payments—and me, too.

But wait. It's still Tuesday afternoon.
And only the first half of that: all the minutes
until 2—which comes at last
and everyone drops what they are doing
if they hadn't already been drifting toward
their lunchboxes, or edging between the parts-racks
in the direction of the caterer's carts
which always appear a few minutes before the hooter
and may be taken on good authority as incontrovertible proof
that 2 o'clock is actually going to arrive.

And this last ten minute break of the day
is when I finally empty my lunchbox and the thermos inside
and put the now lightweight container back on its shelf
and dive into the day's fourth quarter: only 110 minutes.
Also, 20 to 30 minutes before the end I stop
and push a broom around, or just fiddle with something

or maybe fill up various parts-trays with washers
and bolts, or talk to the partsman, climb out of my
coveralls, and generally slack off.
Until the 4 p.m. hooter of hooters
when I dash to the timeclock, a little shoving and pushing
in line, and I'm done. Whew.

But even when I quit
the numbers of the minutes and hours from this shift
stick with me: I can look at a clock some morning
months afterwards, and see it is 20 minutes to 9
—that is, if I'm ever out of bed that early—
and the automatic computer in my head
starts to type out: *20 minutes to 9, that means*
30 minutes to work after 9: you are
50 minutes from the break; 50 minutes
of work, and it is only morning, and it is only
Monday, you poor dumb bastard...

And that's how it goes, round the clock, until a new time
from another job bores its way into my brain.

Garrison

A man is running across Wyoming.
Away out on the high plains,
nothing around him but the wind and sky,
a man runs along the paved shoulder
of the great Interstate crossing Wyoming from west to east.
Cars pass him; the faces of children
stare out of rear windows.
And trucks pull by, the drivers high above the road
watch him run a long way ahead as they approach and go on.

Garrison is running across Wyoming.
He has always run. He ran in military school
and in the Army's summer camps.
"They wanted us to get up at 5:30 A.M.
So at 5 I'd be up doing laps. They couldn't believe it."
He went to college on a scholarship for track.
"I was good, but I wasn't that good.
I never could get into competition. I'd place,
but I think I only won in a meet once or twice.
I just liked to run. We'd have a good time,
me and a few others. I remember one relay
where the first guy on our team was great,
the second guy was good,
then they gave the baton to me.
I ran full out, but I lost most of the lead we had.
When I passed to my friend
he could see we weren't going to win:
he was even slower on that distance than I was.
So he ran one lap
then out of the stadium
into the dressing room
and was sitting outside having showered and changed
when the coach caught up to him.
The coach didn't know what to do.
He'd never seen anybody run right out of a race."

Now Garrison strides down a long hill in the afternoon sun,
his T-shirt plastered to his back, above the pavement,
face contorted with the strain.

"At college," he says,
"I used to run down from the jock dorm
about a mile to a little amusement park
where they had this miniature railroad
parents would take their kids on for rides.
There was a cinder track that paralleled the train tracks
so I'd run on that. Pretty soon
a train would come up behind
and I'd put on a burst of speed
to see if I could beat it.
The guy at the controls of the little engine
would open the throttle
nuh nuh nuh-nuh nuhnuhnuh and I'd tear ahead
trying to do better. People on board
would shout and wave
but I had to leap a couple of ditches
and in any case by the time I ever got to the park
I'd already run a ways so I wasn't exactly fresh.

"One day, though, I got into strip
and drove my car down.
I got out and hid in the bushes
on the further side of the worst ditch.
When the train came around the corner
I leaped out and yelled in the driver's ear
Let's go and took off up the track.
He opened her up *nuh nuh nuh-nuh nuhnuhnuh*
and took off after me, the people
screaming and cheering as he drew closer.
They thought they were helping win the race
but actually they were just sitting there yelling
and he would have gone faster if they weren't aboard.
Anyway, that time we were neck and neck
when we got round to the ditch again."

16 / *The Order in Which We Do Things*

His feet, in Wyoming,
pull the asphalt behind him, stroke after stroke,
breath hauled in and pushed out with his long legs;
eyes blue under the blue sky.

He went to graduate school
in ROTC, studying education. He listened
to what people said about the War
and asked the Army about it,
so they let him go. After that,
he asked his professors about their work, too,
bringing his hound Ralph into classes
and offices, using the dog as a point of reference
in discussing teaching techniques.
He was living then at the edge of town
in a tiny cabin, and running
miles along the country roads
and laps around a tree-lined campus oval.

Until he quit, got a job working demolition,
then in the southern part of the state
went logging. "The only thing political down there,"
he says, "was the Birch Society meetings.
So I'd go along. Mostly it was a good place
to talk about hunting and trade guns and all that.
I'd refuse to take the oath of allegiance
to start the meeting. Freak 'em out.
Told them I was a Commie. Then we'd talk about dogs
and rifles. I kept winning most of the turkey shoots
they had down there, with my old single-shot.
They didn't know what to make of it. I figured
one crazy Commie at a Birch meeting
is better than a dozen films sent out from California.

"I remember one time I was over
talking guns with Billy Hankin.
I saw he had a couple of bumper stickers
on the back of his pickup:

Support Your Right To Bear Arms and
Support Your Local Police. 'Billy,' I said to him,
'you know if they pass a law outlawing guns
it isn't the Communists
who are going to come by to pick up your rifles.
It'll be Sheriff MacLeod.' Next time I saw the truck
the bumper sticker about the police was torn off."

He had enough education credits
to teach remedial subjects in the winters
and he logged, summers. He married
and got his teaching certificate finally,
had a daughter and hurt his back in the woods
so it had to be operated on.
Then his wife left him, and he came apart,
driving west to San Francisco non-stop
in his old jeep, and north into Canada
to a rural teaching job some friends got him.
There, too, he ran
and sat in the bar mourning his marriage
while the jukebox sang *you can't hide
yer cheatin' eyes* and he quit in January
and moved further north
to work as a counselor on a ranch for delinquent boys.
"The kids could go to jail or to the ranch," he says.
"They were some mean little monsters.
A couple of them had been found guilty
of setting cars on fire. Shortly after they got to the ranch
they took off. We got the RCMP after them
and they were picked up in Hazelton.
The Mountie puts them into the back of his car
but one of them opens the door somehow
and zips away up the street. So the cop,
who isn't too bright, leaves one kid in the car
while he runs after the other.

By the time he gets back with the first kid,
sure enough, the other one had the cop car nicely ablaze.

"These kids are real puzzle-factory inmates,
penguins, that's what I call them. One night
a bunch of them got into a fight in the meal hall,
squirting ketchup at each other
and throwing bread around and everything.
I was supposed to be on duty, so I went in there
and didn't pay attention to them
but began kicking over tables, smashing plates and cups,
tipping over chairs. Just went insane.
I looked up after a minute
and saw all the kids huddled into a corner
watching me. 'Now clean this up
and your mess too,' I said
and walked out, and they went to work
and got everything tidy. I just showed them
what it's like when an adult goes nutty.
No good yelling at them or threatening them.
They've had plenty of that.
If a penguin comes at me to hit me
sometimes I'll just wrap my arms around him
so he can't move his
and pick him up and dance with him. He gets really angry
but then he calms down and nobody gets hurt."

Now Garrison is travelling back to Colorado
for a long-delayed compensation hearing about his back.
"I never can do what I want to, Tom," he says
as we drive. "I got out of teaching because
I like to work with my hands. I have to stay in shape:
any job I've been I want to work full out.
But most jobs, you're letting everybody else down
if you work too hard. I like the outdoor stuff at the ranch

but the place is crazy, it's really a jail,
the kids don't want to be there. And there's no women.
I go into town and meet somebody
and fall in love and make a fool of myself.
I don't want to do that. I want to be better to women.
But I don't know how."

His fingers reach up to twist
the thin blond hair above his forehead.
"Tom, who needs us? I mean
I think maybe this is the first time
people like us have been really useless.
What can we work at, give it everything,
that isn't hurting someone else
or adding to the sick way things are going?
What are we good for? Sometimes I honestly wish
I'd gone and fought in the War."

At a rest-stop, he says he wants to stretch,
cramped from riding in the small car.
He changes into strip and starts east down the freeway
while I finish some lunch, check the oil
and drive out after him.
A speck in the distance
at the edge of the highway
Garrison runs as the traffic speeds past him
in the hot day. The only human figure
in the vast panorama
of wind and landscape, a man
is headed for Rawlins,
running across Wyoming,
running towards Jerusalem.

Friday Night in Early September at Morris and Sara Wayman's Farm, Roseneath, Ontario

At dusk, the grey wooden barn
drops anchor near the house
like a huge ship riding at the top of the fields.
On the barn roof, against the lighter part of the sky
pigeons flutter and call. Silence everywhere else
except for a car speeding by on the road.

It's an old barn: inside in the day
the wide beams show adze marks
from when they were squared by hand. Age
is what this ship carries
besides the hay hoisted in each year
to the upper decks
and the cattle loaded aboard below late in the fall.
And she has held other cargo: two years ago
her bins were full of oats; the farmer who rents the land
trucked his crop to Peterborough
to find the cereal manufacturers there wouldn't pay enough
to meet his costs. So he drove back in a rage
and dumped the oats here.

It was always a difficult farm: each inch of it
cut out of the forest; stones down in the fields
had to be levered out each spring before plowing.
Now only beef is grown: the farmer runs his herd
on four such farms owned by city people.
This property was bought when an old woman died.
She had lived in fewer and fewer rooms, sealing off
the upstairs, then parts of the main floor,
until her life was the bedroom and an adjoining kitchen.
The present owners use the place summers and weekends.

This evening, in the dim vegetable garden
the corn is finished, the tomatoes and carrots
are ready for picking. Just before dark
the fields look exhausted,
cropped close by the cattle in their daily tidal drift over the land.
The animals are out of sight now, on the slope of the furthest hill.
At dawn they will be up around the barn again
as it floats into the morning
with the first of the chill air it will haul all winter
already stored in its holds.

White Hand

The chain saw bites into the wood: the faller
is making the undercut
then his back cut.
And when the tree is felled
it is bucked to length,
and later the rigging crew
hauls it out to a landing.
Danger is everywhere: the rotten tops
of snags, or when a cable unexpectedly tightens
or parts, or a log slips from the grapple
and rolls. Shadowed by death, the log is carried by truck
and then perhaps to the world
of water: broomsticks and swifters
and tugs, and on to the mills.

But in the green brush
two hands stay on the chain saw
for months.
The chain cuts into the wood, the heavy saw
is lifted in, jams, is worked free
and lifted into the cut again,
for years. The constant motion
of the engine, the chain,
is sawing too
at the smallest of blood vessels
and nerves: as in the guts of a cat operator,
what in the hand of this man
is shaking free
cannot grow back—white hand,
they call it, the hand gone permanently numb,
useless…

    I take a sheet of paper
and place its sharp corners

in my typewriter roller and turn it,
and around the roller, facing my keys,
appears first the tip
of a man's middle finger, then the tops
of the others, so I type the poem
on the palm of a man's hand, a brother's:
white page
white hand

Silos

Chemical rain
stings the oil-flecked surface of the sea.

Inland, a strip of forest infected by blight,
dyed orange with a retardant

dropped by helicopter,
surrounds a sterile lake.

Here the silos
are emplaced.

Inside these, below ground, men
with the faces of machines

forget everything they learned about the sun,
leaf through manuals filled with initials and

numbers, searching for the coded designations for
death. They have brothers under the ocean

in submersible cylinders
holding more of the burning fodder

meant to feed death. And above
in the ultraviolet sky

is the remote thunder of airborne silos
packed with electronic delivery programs

for the fertilizers of death.
Yet bears

still walk our forest paths
down each evening

to the landfill, browsing
among the crushed tins and papers, disposable diapers,

the abandoned televisions.
Deer lie along the highway ditches

near portions of robin, porcupine, grouse
on the pavement. Our masters

have established their rights to the earth:
gut it, package and sell it

and get out. In their humming silos
they store what they save

of this harvest
as if to ensure no report of themselves,

of what they do
passes into any history. And they ask us

to help improve the planet, they urge us
don't litter

Paper, Scissors, Stone

An executive's salary for working with paper
beats the wage in a metal shop operating shears
which beats what a gardener earns arranging stone.

But the pay for a surgeon's use of scissors
is larger than that of a heavy equipment driver removing stone
which in turn beats a secretary's cheque for handling paper.

And, a geologist's hours with stone
nets more than a teacher's with paper
and definitely beats someone's time in a garment factory with
      scissors.

In addition: to manufacture paper,
you need stone to extract metal to fabricate scissors
to cut the product to size.
To make scissors you must have paper to write out the specs
and a whetstone to sharpen the new edges.
Creating gravel, you require the scissor-blades of the crusher
and lots of order forms and invoices at the office.

Thus I believe there is a connection
between things
and not at all like the hierarchy of winners
of a child's game.
When a man starts insisting
he should be paid more than me
because he's more important to the task at hand,
I keep seeing how the whole process collapses
if almost any one of us is missing.
When a woman claims she deserves more money
because she went to school longer,
I remember the taxes I paid to support her education.
Should she benefit twice?

Then there's the guy who demands extra
because he has so much seniority
and understands his work so well
he has ceased to care, does as little as possible,
or refuses to master the latest techniques
the new-hires are required to know.
Even if he's helpful and somehow still curious
after his many years—
again: nobody does the job alone.

Without a machine to precisely measure
how much sweat we each provide
or a contraption hooked up to electrodes in the brain
to record the amount we think,
my getting less than him
and more than her
makes no sense to me.
Surely whatever we do at the job
for our eight hours—as long as it contributes—
has to be worth the same.

And if anyone mentions
this is a nice idea but isn't possible,
consider what we have now:
everybody dissatisfied, continually grumbling and disputing.
No, I'm afraid it's the wage system that doesn't function
except it goes on
and will
until we set to work to stop it

with paper, with scissors, and with stone.

The Face of Jack Munro

1

In the November rain we walked
back and forth
across a driveway which led
to a parking lot:
four of us—two support staff,
two faculty—and we stood aside,
dripping, if a car tried to nose in past us
or emerged. The wet wind
chilled our faces
and hands, as we paced
on the asphalt flowing with a thin wash
of runoff, so a clamminess
also rose into our soaked boots.
Cardboard signs
that hung from our neck with string
were wrapped in clear plastic
down which the water rolled, while we held them
against the gusts of the storm.
Once somebody from the main entrance
showed up with a bag of doughnuts
a supporter had donated
and Dale volunteered to go for coffees
which we eventually drank,
holding the hot styrofoam cups
in our hands. The rain
seeped through the seams of my coat
after a while, dampening my shirt
and then my skin. In the culvert
under the driveway
the water sang, pouring through
into a ditch
lined with tall weeds and grasses,

some paper litter,
in the cold rain.

2

I worked that autumn with Dale
Zieroth, Maureen Shaw,
John Waters, John Reed
and others—just names to you,
probably. All of us were employed
to instruct
what we knew.

But those who administered us
and those who had hired
them
wanted us to know
only a prescribed amount.
We were not to notice
that in the air
a sour odour
was leaking, as if from a refinery
upwind. It was a stench
of sulphur, of worn dollar bills,
of half-digested steak
belched through false smiles
at the poor.

After a while, everyone smelled it.
Some pretended it wasn't there.

3

This stink
arose from fear.

One gang of liars
had been elected, and to them
our lives were mirrors:
they saw evil.
So they strode into welfare dentists' offices
and shut these down.
They ordered the demolition
of wheelchair access ramps
and their replacement by stairs.
They informed battered women
fortitude is a virtue.
They advised the young without jobs
to eat less.
They ordered tenants
to register with a central bureau
so files could be opened on our suitability
to be housed.
They said discrimination of any type
is acceptable
as long as no harm is intended.
They announced everyone paid by the public
except themselves
could be fired without cause.

They put a price on the highways
and handed these over to their friends.
They evaluated the firehalls
and the hospitals for the retarded
and offered these in the bond markets
of the East. They enforced an embargo
on food allocated to the hungry
and paid for enormous scaffoldings
to be erected in the largest cities
for purposes no one could fathom.
They told civic officials
their jurisdictions would henceforth be limited

to bird inventories and traffic signal maintenance.
And that these functions
would be assigned
to a select list of corporations.
They invited purchasers to submit bids
on clearing the wolves and elk from our forests.
They advised farmers
there is no crop more vital to human need
than mortgages.

Whatever was owned in common
they closed, ruined, or gave away.
Our trees could not be cut and milled quickly enough,
so they issued permits for logs
to be dragged directly overseas.
This was still too slow: they gave grants
to research companies
to investigate the towing of whole coastal islands
offshore for processing.
Money witheld from schools
went to fund extra tracking of railroads
to haul ore more rapidly to dumps by the ocean.
When customers balked
at taking entire mountains for free
a program was initiated to offer compensation
for the removal of these detriments to the environment.
The government announced their intention
to sell the rivers, sell streams,
sell the water still in the clouds.
And they introduced tax increases
to pay the costs of implementing
these measures.

4

But we drew a line
and walked it.

First there were rallies and marches—
forty thousand of us
making a giant stadium pulse and hum
with protest, banners, shouts
and leaflets.
And strange events
resulted: other liars, who had always claimed
at election time to be on our side
vanished
leaving only their campaign posters
which they asked us to erect on our lawns
in four or five years
if there were still candidates and elections.
At our union meetings, now
disunity
was general. Some were opposed
to any action, others
demanded it;
some were terrified of changes
we might make,
others of the changes already decreed.

Yet women and men
stood one by one
and spoke
and we argued and
voted
and together we constructed a line.

So the union executives
had to announce a Plan:
little by little, they said,
groups of us could emerge
and stand in the rain.

Tens of thousands of us
that November

did—the clerks who issue government
liquor permits, the bridge crews
from the Highways yards,
maintenance people from colleges,
teachers of physical education
and French, data processors
from the government insurance bureaus.

While we grew
the newspapers and televisions
appeared frantic: they hired extra scribblers
to be sure every person who wished to cross our line
was interviewed in depth.
Columns and editorials
brayed about chaos
but eighty thousand human beings
now stood outside their workplace
and not a rock was thrown,
not a single tire slashed,
nobody even complained of being shoved.

>   Yet there were those
>   who pushed past us
>   into the empty buildings.
>   Not many did this
>   and in some places none,
>   but some.

No one called them scabs.
A scab is a crust of dead matter
in a wound. These people were
leeches, desperate to suck nourishment for themselves
from a stricken host, leeches
scurrying to live
in an open sore,
   leeches unwilling to join,

    to help their neighbours
    but eager to share our gains
    if we won.

And after two weeks
we began to win.
The people drenched on the line
learned to laugh at the sneering
of the television, refused to believe any more
in the newspaper,
trusted each other and the words of approval
from additional citizens who arrived each morning
to walk beside us.
The politicians and news teams
became increasingly frenzied,
they found economists to forecast
the end of the earth,
on our line
people almost burst into song.

The frightened among us
redoubled their efforts:
"Let's accept the situation. The smell
will disappear in time." Or:
"Let's find a perfume—new words
to describe what they are doing to us
that don't stink so badly."

But by the second Sunday,
poised to go out
were others of us:
the next day, municipal parks board employees,
drivers of garbage trucks, drainage
inspectors, and later the same week
the men and women who staff the cafeterias
on the coastal ferries

and the deckhands, bus drivers
and those who repair transit vehicles
and clean them, and some days after that
all but a designated core of hospital workers.

The world was full of love.

5

In our midst, though,
was error
greater than the leeches:
a cancer
few could see.

At this hour
in history, when it was clear to anyone
that our daily work
enables the world to function, and who
are parasites

there arose

a man called Jack Munro

—a burly man,
elected to represent the roar
and hustle of the sawmills, of the plywood
and fibreboard plants, the horns and machine-noise
of the logging sidehills, a man
come into the quiet offices
of the union, the structures
that whispered to him
power,
the rooms where bargains are made
by shirts and ties,

the conference corridors
where lives are traded;

—this man
eaten inside by the invisible cancer
now suddenly shouldered past
those who had claimed they were leading us.
He whistled for a government aircraft
which arrived for him that Sunday,
and he soared
high over the rock-firm picket lines,
far above the panic filling the thoughts
of owners and company vice-presidents and personnel managers,
away up beyond our certain success.
And when Jack Munro descended
he entered the Kelowna house
of the man who headed
this government of death.

And the two men shook hands, because this other man
was also very sick with the cancer.
Then Jack Munro
took out his wallet
and placed it on a table.

The other man
took out his wallet, too,
and placed it beside Munro's.
The leather cases
were almost identical,
each thick with crisp bills
and uncashed cheques.
And while Jack Munro sat
and stuffed snacks into his fat jowls,
the two wallets
commenced negotiations.
Both wallets agreed

the moment was perilous,
that authority must be maintained
and that for this to occur
one side must win and the other lose.
They agreed
the present actions of the many
in daring to resist
were more dangerous to authority
than the actions of the few in oppressing.
So it was concluded
that Jack Munro was to order the hierarchy below him
to close down our lines,
that in return for nothing
Jack Munro was to announce our defeat,
to inform us we had obtained through our efforts
nothing.

And in return for our compliance
the government would be free
to implement whatever it desired.
But we should be grateful
because at least
the usual authority would be preserved.

And the mouths of the two wallets smiled,
and the two wallets shook hands
for the news photographers
and Jack Munro was carried again
high into the atmosphere
from where he started to issue his commands

and now we saw the cancer,
saw how deep the cancer had spread
among us,
and were told Jack Munro's orders
were non-debatable by us,
were told voting by us on this issue
was irrelevant

and we did not know what to do
and we were lost.

6

Thus Jack Munro
sold out the woodyard
by the creek, sold out the school bus
letting the children off by the lane
up to a ranch, sold out the waiting room
at Emergency, the empty job boards
at the employment centres.
Jack Munro sold out
the regional museum,
the women and men anxious
for an opening at daycare,
sold out the grapple operator
on the landing, sold out the secretaries
headed for lunch, the gill netters, instrument
technicians, welders
and geologists.
He sold out the palsied
and the athlete, sold out the accountant at her desk
and the man wild in the street
who knows he has lost control.

Jack Munro sold out this province
house by house,
district by district,
kilometre by kilometre.

7

How could it occur
that direction of our struggle

shrank to one man?
How is it we took up the fight
convinced of the good will of those
we put above us?

>   Those days in November I felt
>   the presence of
>   another room alongside this one,
>   another field and sky
>   beside this meadow
>   and air.
>   It seemed we had built
>   a passageway to that crystal life,
>   a door which took shape
>   from our careful daily acts of
>   defiance.
>   But we left a few to keep
>   that opening for us
>   and when we tried to cross through
>   we learned they had taken it away.

What Jack Munro accomplished
now hangs over every hour.
At each press conference
to explain the curtailment of more liberties
the government spokesperson stares at us
with the eyes
of Jack Munro.
At the bargaining sessions
where negotiators from management
demand we be punished, earn less,
live less well,
the employers' representatives speak
using the voice
of Jack Munro.
The supervisor delivering layoff notices,
the tribunal refusing to hear the eviction appeal,
the businessmen and women gloating over dinner

at the news of the reduction of
payments to the single unemployed
—all share a face
puffy with greed and fright and satisfaction,
the face of
Jack Munro.

> A malignancy
> bitter and deep
> has carved a bully's cunning
> into the convolutions of Jack Munro's brain.
> But the spores that brought him this tumour,
> this anti-democracy, this fear
> originated elsewhere
> and have taken some root
> in us, too.
> How else can we forget each time
> that decisions must be made by ourselves
> and not left to the leaderships,
> officers,
> steering committees?
> For centuries
> this cancer has taught us to obey,
> spoken for us, told us what to think.

Yet we have always
breathed
on our own, at least.
And our emancipation
is as natural
and complex
as that simple motion:
inhale
      exhale
bringing the life that is oxygen
to the blood
bearing away the wastes

like injustice,
which other living things
transform into their wholesome existences.
So there is a use
even for a great wrong
on this planet
in this process
of mutual
and perfect
solidarity
we still have to devise

for ourselves.

A Cursing Poem: This Poem Wants Gordon Shrum to Die
1971

This poem wants to hurt another person.
This poem wants another person to die.
It wants him to suddenly stumble
feel a sharp pain just under the belly
a harsh pain, one that rips him so hard inside that he shits himself.
The poem wants him to become dizzy
feel a rush of sweat on the face
to begin to shiver, and have to be helped into bed.
The poem wants his teeth to chatter, wants him to throw up
gasping for air, wants mucus to pour from his nose and mouth.
It wants him to die in the night.

This poem wants Gordon Shrum to die.
First because despite all his company's rules and tariffs
despite every regulation they tell the press they apply
his company turned off the heat and light in the house.
They did this without warning, when the temperature was forty
      degrees by day
and the nights begin at four o'clock.
So that after working all day, the body could come home
to a room of black ice.

So after straining all day at the jobsite, with the fingers
numb at the hammer and slipping under the weight of the heavy
      boards
after the back was twisted trying to hoist the load of a wheelbarrow
the rest of the body could return to darkness and cold.

This poem also wants Gordon Shrum to die
because his company charges twenty-five cents every day
for the bus to carry you to work. And because you must
pay the same every evening to wait in the cold
to be jerked and stopped and jerked and stopped
all the way back to the house. Fifty cents a day

taken out of the dollars squeezed from the body's labour
so at the end of the day, the body can be hauled to where it stays
    overnight
can enter the black bedrooms, be lit by a candle
and eat bread and cold milk.

Lastly the poem wants Gordon Shrum to die
because at a meeting he reached over to my friend Mark Warrior
and smacked him in the mouth.
He was charged and duly acquitted
because Mark was shouting out at the time how the French
were finally getting off their knees
and striking back at the bullies that push them, at the men like
    Shrum
—whom Mark didn't name.

But whom I name, with his bureaucrats and service division
his credit office and transportation system. Him, and
every other animal who is gnawing away at our lives.
May before they die
they know what it is like to be cold, may the cold eat into them
may they live so they cough all night and can't sleep
and have to get up the next morning for work just the same.
May the joints of their bodies swell with their labour
and their backs ache. And before they die
may they know deeply, to the inside of their stomachs
the meaning of a single word:
unemployment. May they understand it
as the nourishment a man gets by scraping the calendar over a
    pan for a meal.

May they have a future with nothing in it
but unemployment; may they end on welfare.

May they have to travel by bus
to get their welfare. May they wake in the night and realize
that for the rest of their lives they will never eat together
all the things they love: steak and wine and hot corn.
They will never have these together again until they die.
May they die on welfare.
And may the Lord God *Jesus* have mercy on their souls.

The Poet

Taken from A Checklist to Aid in the Detection of Learning Disabilities

Loses his position on worksheet or page in textbook
May speak much but makes little sense
Cannot give clear verbal instructions
Does not understand what he reads
Does not understand what he hears
Cannot handle "yes-no" questions

Has great difficulty interpreting proverbs
Has difficulty recalling what he ate for breakfast, etc.
Cannot tell a story from a picture
Cannot recognize visual absurdities

Has difficulty classifying and categorizing objects
Has difficulty retaining such things as
addition and subtraction facts, or multiplication tables
May recognize a word one day and not the next

Defective Parts of Speech: Official Errata

Where it says *welfare* read *suffering*
"The seasonally-adjusted rate of suffering
fell one per cent last month."
Where it says *defense* read *suffering*
"The Department of Suffering confirmed Friday
the shipment of $1 billion in new tanks and helicopters
to friendly governments in Latin America."
Where it says *productivity* read *suffering*
"Canadian industry must increase the suffering of its employees
at least 12 per cent this year."
Where it says *co-operation* read *suffering*
"The administration requires the suffering of every citizen
to see us through these difficult times."

Where it says *efficiency* read *suffering*
Where it says *management* read *suffering*
Where it says suffering read *defeat*

Did I Miss Anything?

Question frequently asked by students after missing a class

Nothing. When we realized you weren't here
we sat with our hands folded on our desks
in silence, for the full two hours

> Everything. I gave an exam worth
> 40 per cent of the grade for this term
> and assigned some reading due today
> on which I'm about to hand out a quiz
> worth 50 per cent

Nothing. None of the content of this course
has value or meaning
Take as many days off as you like:
any activities we undertake as a class
I assure you will not matter either to you or me
and are without purpose

> Everything. A few minutes after we began last time
> a shaft of light descended and an angel
> or other heavenly being appeared
> and revealed to us what each woman or man must do
> to attain divine wisdom in this life and
> the hereafter
> This is the last time the class will meet
> before we disperse to bring this good news to all people on earth

Nothing. When you are not present
how could something significant occur?

> Everything. Contained in this classroom
> is a microcosm of human existence
> assembled for you to query and examine and ponder
> This is not the only place such an opportunity has been gathered
>
> but it was one place
>
> And you weren't here

The Man Who Logged the West Ridge

The man who logged the West Ridge,
unlike the person who owns it,
has his home on the Valley floor.
The money this man got
for taking away the West Ridge's trees
paid a crew, made payments on a truck
and a skidder, reduced a mortgage, bought food
and a new outboard
and was mailed off to the owner.

So the fir and larch and pine
of the Ridge, its deer and coyote,
snails and hummingbirds,
were dollars for a brief time,
then were gone from our Valley.
Fair enough. While the logging was in progress
the man stood on the new road along the slope
to shout at a pickup full of people from below
over the howls of the saws
and the surging diesels:
I don't have to talk to you.
I am leaving a few trees. I don't have to do that.
Bug me, and I'll level this place completely.

Once the West Ridge was empty,
the owner put the land up for sale.
Remaining that close to the sky
is slash, and the churned soil,
heaps of cable and plastic oil containers
and a magazine of photographs
of young women's breasts and vaginas
that got passed around one lunchhour
and looked at, while everyone ate their sandwiches
resting against some logs. Nobody wanted to keep

the publication, not even the one who brought it,
so its pages lie on the earth near a torn-out stump,
the paper shrivelling into rain.

And the man who logged the Ridge
is finished with it, although he and the rest of us
constantly traverse its lowest levels
where the lane winds between our houses
and fields
toward the highway. Yet the Ridge
is not finished with the Valley
—its shadow continues to slip down its creekbeds
every afternoon
darkening the land as far as the river
while the other side still receives the sun.
That shadow, once of a forest,
now is born from an absence, from money,
from eight weeks' work.
We live each day shadowed by the Ridge,
neighbours of the man who cut it down.

For William Stafford (1914–1993)

Travelling in the dusk, I hit a deer
on the Monashee Highway west of the Needles ferry

A brown blur
passed above the hood

then the metallic gasp and
thud of two vehicles that collide

The truck drove on
all the dashboard gauges normal

while I steered to the shoulder
and braked, the motor idling

On either side, forested mountains
bore their silent February snows

I rounded the front of the truck
and stopped: it had been caved in

as though I had struck a post
—the bumper bent outwards

to a semicircle, grill smashed
piercing the radiator, coolant leaking down

in weak streams
One headlight shone ahead

but the other was wrenched 90 degrees
through shattered glass

I mounted again
and swung the engine's final minutes

across the asphalt and back
to see the deer

which lay facing east
dead

one eye aimed toward me
like a rifle

or a gold coin burnished to a flash
or the illumination device

of a vessel
from a different sun

War on a Round Planet

In the aircraft over a foreign country
a young man from Weyburn, Saskatchewan
throws a toggle switch

and a metal cylinder detaches from the wing
and falls
By this act

the man in the plane
authorizes the destruction of most of a block
of downtown Weyburn—a movie theatre, a bank

a small grocery store with a photography studio
above, a vacant building for lease
—plus several homes in the adjacent street

Fourteen people die
immediately, including six children, and
a woman and a man die later of wounds

despite being evacuated to hospital in Regina
A young woman is blinded
and two men lose a leg and arm respectively

Of the thirty-four other wounded
twelve are off work for more than six weeks
and one man never returns to his former

occupation—farming
No children are orphaned but
several families are reorganized

due to sadness
Eight people suffer some permanent hearing loss
or significant reduction in the use of one or more limbs

and a woman begins a series of outpatient treatments
for mental dysfunction, eventually resulting
in permanent institutionalization

On the ground below the aircraft
a soldier's rifle recoils into his shoulder
At once two shadows depart from the barrel

The echo of the shot races backwards along the sights
around the young man's body
and continues in a straight-line trajectory

over the horizon behind him
Simultaneously, the bullet
spirals forward

in the direction the weapon points
Influenced by a force
more fundamental than gravity

the projectile maintains a constant elevation
as it traverses woodlands and grassy meadows
oceans and orchards

rises over mountain ridges
and descends again above
vineyards or rice paddies

terraced along valley walls
At a speed incalculably swifter than light
the bullet approaches and passes its echo

proceeding in the reverse direction
and homes in on the soldier who released it
who still kneels in the position

from which he fired
"Incoming!" is the last sound
the young man comprehends

Cup

Because of heavy painkillers
administered to my father
or a deep dream,
before he died he called out from a doze in his wheelchair:
Take, take it.
His tone was desperate, so I stepped closer
to reassure: *It's all right. You were asleep.*
What's the matter?
His eyes now gaped at his world:
the curtain isolating him from the other bed here,
a portable commode, his wheeled tray
holding an untouched lunch of broth and jello.
Then he recognized me and said:
I was drinking a cup of coffee
with nowhere to put it down.
His voice was anxious and bewildered so I soothed:
It was just a dream; don't worry.
But he said: *Take it from me,*
anyway. After a moment
I reached across his lap to seize
a cup of nothing
which I held to my chest as I straightened again.
My father smiled slightly
at the oddity of this event
and slept. Thus his cup
passed to me.

Epithalamium for a Former Lover

Let her rose stems droop,
And the blooms be leprous and dulled.

Let the place of ceremony have
Off-green cement block walls, unrelieved by ornament,

And be lit by one fluorescent fixture
Whose sole functioning tube flickers and hums.

May the closest parking lot
Be three blocks away

And the wedding party drenched by a sudden hailstorm
As they scurry toward the building.

May an old girlfriend of the groom's
Appear uninvited,

Obviously stoned, who talks loudly and incomprehensibly
To those seated on either side of her

Even once the ritual starts.
Let the presiding official

Be so elderly he must be assisted to the front
Dressed inappropriately in a stained sweatsuit

And during a rambling preliminary discourse
Refer to the nuptial couple

By the wrong names several times
In the course of arguments intended to prove

The area has been repeatedly visited by alien spacecraft.
Even when a member of the audience

Manages to blurt out a gentle correction
Concerning the name of the bride and groom,

The official, once he finally comprehends the issue,
Commits the same error seconds later.

Let the ex-girlfriend's commentary on the incident
So provoke the groom's Uncle Reggie, already largely drunk,

That he opines she should shut her face.
May her reply, involving unique and imaginative profanity,

Inspire Reggie to leap from his seat
And attempt to resolve their divergent views

On acceptable wedding decorum
By physical means.

Let chairs around the dispute
Be tipped over as shoving and pushing commence

And someone yells out the police have been notified.
May the police take nearly an hour to respond to the call

During which a cluster of the younger guests
Forms around the antagonists in an attempt to restrain them,

While the rest of the assembly
Forms small groups engaged in spirited debate

Over the merits of the semifinal contenders of some sport,
Or whether Alex has a chance with Lucia

On Days of Our Lives.
Let moments before the arrival of a patrolman

The presiding official announce he is late for a different appointment
And shuffle out of the hall

Considerately leaving his paperwork behind.
So when the constable shows up

He must be importuned into completing the ceremony
Which, after handcuffing the ex-girlfriend,

Loading her into the rear of his cruiser,
And ordering Uncle Reggie off the premises,

He does. Then as everyone crowds around the now-united pair,
Let the cell phone of the bride's brother

Inform the gathering
The house where the reception is to be held

Has just been burglarized, with most of the wedding gifts
Stolen, along with a packet of congratulatory communications

Temporarily stored in a
Silver-plated gravy tureen,

Including a postcard I sent—with six cents postage due—
That wishes the two, however briefly their marriage might last,

All the joy they deserve.

Calgary

A slag heap of dollars
with portions hidden behind facades
designed by famous international architects
down on their luck
—an immense tailings mound of money
toward which fleets of tanker trucks
sloshed full of additional cash
stream to disgorge

Two inches of fresh snow overnight
at mid-May

A buffalo standing, head lowered, defeated
as though formed of suburban ornamental brush
in a yard beside the traffic stalled at the corner of
32nd Avenue and Shaganappi
just east of Market Mall

                Cigarette smoke
churning onto the street from the bar doorways
where according to the police crime tally
young white men stab each other every second midnight
alternating with Vietnamese gangs whose preference for disputes is
pistols and long guns

                A metropolis in which
nobody is born
permitting the demolition of half the hospitals
and the resultant tax saving applied
to subsidize private plastic surgery clinics

                        A blizzard
pushing southward in June, that drags down
limbs of the ornamental cherry
and suffocates the narcissus

                    A Dodge pickup
hauling two dead cows, heads lolling out the tailgate
in an attempt to hold at a distance
the customary flock of spoiler-equipped sports cars
quivering inches behind whatever moves along asphalt
in their anxiety to be anyplace else

                         Frost on the lawns
one July morning

               Sour gas corporation CEOs
awarded annual remuneration
four hundred times the average wage of company employees
who still insist they are generously paid
A person who lives off investments
complaining about the sloth of the poor

                              Icy wind from the mountains
August 13th, snowflakes suspended in mid-air
from an overcast, melting when they eventually descend

Swaths of tract houses eating the Prairie
at each cardinal point: acres of treeless bloated dwellings
that seep outward from the shopping centers

                                 Sleet
in early September, the streets whitening

as the Bow River curls quietly through
wafting its suicides and abandoned mattresses
toward Hudson's Bay, lower trunks of the cottonwood
and aspen that line its route
wrapped in wire to discourage the presence of beaver
and thus demonstrate efficient management of the biosphere

To the north, the featureless hump of Nose Hill Park
rears over its expanding ring of freeways
—bleak tombstone for what failed to thrive

Postmodern 911

The speaker at the podium is in the midst of rattling off quotes
from several critical theorists as definitive proof
that neither language nor history permit
definitive statements or authorities.
I leap from my seat and stride forward.
As I approach he turns toward me, face puzzled
above his lecture notes
so I hit him twice in the mouth.
His papers fly off the lectern. Uproar in the audience
though nobody utters anything coherent. My hand hurts.
"What are you doing?" he manages, having stepped back a couple of paces,
fingers tenderly feeling his jaw. "Are you completely
nuts?"

    I let him have it in the gut: *doosh doosh.*
When he quits gasping, where he thrashes around on the floor,
I bend over him. "Here's my cell phone. Likely you'll want to call the cops.
I know you just told us reality is strictly a function
of the beholder. But I bet you and I agree
this cell phone is real."

    He glares up at me.
I tap in the famous numbers, proffer the device again
which he snatches. I've activated the speakerphone function
so both sides are audible.

    "Postmodern 911."

"I've been physically attacked by a lunatic, and need help immediately.
I'm in lecture room ST 407, which is — "

    "You mean you *believe* you've been attacked.
Truth, you'll be interested to learn, is entirely relative.
The consequences of such relativity are manifold, including — "

"No, damn it, a moron came right out of the audience
and smacked me for no good reason. He — "

    "Now, I'm sure there are competing narratives."
    The tone via the speaker sounds bored.
    "Multiple interpretations of any construct or happening, however,
    enormously enrich the human experience.
    Of course, if you can legitimately define yourself
    as colonized, discriminated against, or
    identified as Other with respect to — "

"You don't understand.
This prick came out of nowhere and — "

    "Ah, to *you* his origins may constitute 'nowhere',
    as you so smugly refer to it. Perhaps his actions,
    if such actually occurred, constitute
    a trope of tangibly, as it were, writing back to — "

"Metaphor has nothing to do with it.
I've been assaulted. I demand — "

    "Your characterization of experience is far too linear.
    Listen to the following text, and I'm sure
    you'll find its non-narrative structure and accretive compositional
        strategy
    will problematize your description of events and force you
    to more accurately comprehend your situation:
    Yellow plastic kettles of the environment
    condense Bakhtinian anti-logic pliers into — "

"The *police*. Get me the fucking *police*.
This asshole is trying to kill me."

    "I'm afraid reality is more ambiguous
    than postulated by your gendered, probably homophobic,
    probably logocentric world view. See — "

I duck as he throws the cell phone at my head,
scrambles to his feet and adopts a defensive stance:
fists up, fear in his eyes. I consider decking him once more,
when a man wearing a tie appears at my elbow,
the scholar who introduced today's talk.
"That's really all the time we have for this,"
the new arrival proposes in a timorous voice.
To his surprise I nod,
shake him by the hand.

Mt. Gimli Pashtun

                    I

At the start, the trail pushes through alder thickets
    along a creek, then crosses the stream bed
    on two logs with metal mesh affixed for grip. After that
    the path is relentless in its climb: switchback
    after switch-
    back up the wooded ridge,
                        boot by boot
    also scrambling under a fallen trunk
    or over as huckleberries
    swell along the steep route, the forest's species
    changing. The trail eventually lifts amid
    rock ledges, cone-shaped alpine fir
    and stunted brush

                    while the immense black mound
    of Gimli's summit
    is visible between the trees—kruppelholtz branches
    shrivelled by the snows, Engelmann spruce boughs
    seared and malformed by frost—

    until the woods are gone: the path traverses
    an open country
    of tilted inclines of dusty earth
    and stones, sparse grass tufts. The route
    ambles around and atop boulders
    of a scree slope, the trail marked by
    low stacks of rocks.

                    Beside the path,
the mountainside falls away
    into a drainage below: a slanted field of tundra,
    a few clusters of evergreens,

two ponds. Pika watch, squeak and
dart. Gimli's granite ridge
fills the horizon to the north, three hundred metres aloft.
At the eastern end of the cornice, the summit mass
rears a further thousand metres.

II

A loss thrums in the soil here,
vibrates in the cold alpine wind.

Here the Pashtuns blown apart, or maimed
by bullets released in the name of this country

now dwell,
together with the uniformed young men

shuffled into earth in a box
borne by eight of their own, or returned to us

alive but changed.
               All that grows
  in this harsh silence of stones

    grows in the scant weeks clear of snow:
    roots reach to grasp a mountain

    of black dust. To the east, south, west,
    seried bells of blued peaks

    —chop of shore-broken waves—
    toll through the emptiness.

Those who rule us have sent
men and women with our money

and in our name
to kill to protect a corruption

struggling against another corruption. Our lawmakers
have proclaimed as enemy

a force our side once armed to destroy
a third corruption, whose politicians promised,

as do those who now hold the capital,
to pave roads, build schools for women,

curtail opium shipments.
       When a bear

 stands on the trail to block the way,
 her head lifted, tilting side to side

 to scent us, or black fur is abruptly evident
 descending the slope

 toward us, the future
we are given

cannot be predicted or justified.
Achievements, skills, insights

mean nothing to the unreasonable menace
advancing in the icy air:

our government's insistence that they
—that we—have always represented virtue,

that our peaceful heritage
affords our troops the right

to establish fields of fire,
that torture, the stoning of apostates

and adulteresses are our ally's culture,
meriting respect, while our soldiers, each equipped

with expensive armor, communication
devices, night vision goggles, cunningly designed

weaponry, combat clothing and boots
are welcomed

by men and women whose bodies
are wrapped in ragged cloth, who lack shoes.

 The unfairness of the bear's power.
 No protest short of retreat
 or violence suffices
 to counter its presence in our lives.

III

An alien death has been brought
to these mountains. Foot patrols, tank squadrons,
radio calls for other men to kill from the air
—all bedecked with the symbols
of this country—echo among the peaks' vistas of
innumerable summits, roadless forest.

        In the serenity
 above treeline
 a spreading stain bleaches half the sky.
 To the south, amid dim cloud-mounds,
 are flashes of light: detonations
 of an improvised
 innocence.

            near Slocan, B.C.

Air Support

A dropped school falls through air,
turning slowly as debris
pours from windows: a contrail of papers and books
streams upwards thousands of metres
alongside computers, chairs, desks that tumble amid
woodworking equipment, lockers, maps,
basketballs, stage curtains

                              all aimed
toward tiny huts far below—a brushy hillside's
cluster of subsistence farms
reportedly harboring armed men: fenced yards
with a few chickens, one cow, an ancient horse eyeing
six rows of parched vegetables.

                              Above the school
while it descends,
another follows, and beyond that, nearly invisible,
a third floats as the fighter-bomber arcs
away, and a second jet drones into position.
The pilot of the first, now on the mission's homeward leg,
reaches down in his cockpit
toward a thermos of hot coffee.

On the ground, hospitals released
in the initial attack wave
erupt sequentially into plumes of fire and dust
as the buildings land: operating tables,
obstetric wards, wheelchairs shatter into shrapnel,
the jagged particles racing outward amid the roiling smoke
to slice through mud walls, animal flesh, stone fences,
human lives that cling to the shaking
shuddering earth
while they clutch forty-year-old rifles

or axes, or the hand of a two-year-old
below the flash of wing
very distant
in the blue-and-white sky.

Whistle
Tunisia, Egypt, Canada

At the threshold of hearing:
a slight wheezy sound

almost inaudible when
        an entire shift, one hundred and twenty-five men and women
        —twelve of us with fifteen-year long-service pins
        and another thirty with ten-year certificates—
        are ordered to assemble in the lunchroom
        to be told by the Human Resources manager
        the company has taken away our jobs

A tiny background sibilance
        as somebody asks about the news report
        on the huge bonuses awarded the day before to the company's
                executives
        despite the fifth consecutive quarter of losses
        If the corporation didn't offer this level of management
                remuneration,
        we are informed, *it couldn't attract the best and brightest*

A faint tone
that from time to time seems drowned out by
official pronouncements of "labour peace" or
"truth and reconciliation," or by a local conglomerate's purchase of
a sports franchise, in support of which
you can yell, and spend your money on stadium tickets
or replicas of jerseys worn by those players receiving the largest salaries

Yet this muted whistling, always present,
can rise a few decibels
        —as when no rice is available
        or no water, or even when cutbacks to health services
        necessitated by the need to finance an
        international exposition, or overseas military excursion

  mean the average wait in a bed placed in the jammed hospital
    corridors
  before a patient can be moved to a ward
  now stretches from four to six days
The low warbling becomes more shrill
  when a thousand men and women
  push into a hearing room to oppose
  the diversion of a river on behalf of a private contractor
  to generate power for a resort development

  The venture is approved
  regardless
and the noise splutters
almost to silence

But the steady thread of sound, commonly less than a whisper,
is a reassurance to many, an irritation to others,
a threat to a few

because there are also moments the whistle swells in volume
to a level people can't endure
  and run into the streets
  Some men and women clutch sticks
  with cardboard attached bearing words,
  and some carry sticks machined to
  clubs, or metal shafts fashioned into
  gun barrels

  When the noise becomes entirely deafening
    certain men and women can't continue to stay any longer
    in palaces, or chambers of assembly
    This racket alters
    various domestic and community priorities
    perhaps for a few days
    or a decade

And if the tone subsides again

        so wealthy individuals breathe relief
      while the majority of us resume cursing the bus schedule
      or the shift schedule
      or the quality of the season's
      new television offerings,
the whistle, though scarcely discernible,
perseveres:
the tinnitus of the world

The White Dogs

Snow on the riverbank
and on the ice that edged the current.
The track ahead was white,
and the hills shuttering the valley,
white, as I glided northward,
skimming and poling through forest

                          until behind me,
very close: abrupt baying and barking
so I turned and
two white hounds
paced and jostled just beyond my reach,
fangs and jaws expelling knife after knife of sound
at me. Their heads were higher than my waist,
while under the belly of one great animal
a row of teats were shocking in their blackness.
As both dogs snapped continually
in the burning wood of their noise, I was determined to resist
with pole blade and boots.

                    Yet I spoke softly to them
and they quieted, churning the snow with feet and claws,
but their manner was the false politeness of power
feigning courtesy, an assured superior
that finds a mocking humor in the pretense that
the comfort or ideas of a victim matter: a fatal game
whose rules I did not know,
that the animals perhaps did not know,
but both sides knowing one misstep by me
would trigger an onslaught.

                    After some minutes of this truce,
I kicked into motion again. The pair
watched me leave.

                              Returning in the dusk,
I saw a man afoot headed toward me. I stopped the walker—
a bearded man with an eye patch—to ask
whose were the hounds. He said they were frequently encountered
on the trail, though I had travelled here a dozen times before
and never seen them. *They respond according to*
those who meet them, the man informed me.
If you're agitated or aggressive, so are they.
If you're calm, they are too. I thanked him
and we resumed our separate journeys
into night. What I heard the white bitch say to me
was: *The fears you have clutched to yourself all your life*
are useless. Whether you are afraid or not
you are going to die. Her mate or brother
had sounded agreement. If I had carried the cold oiled metal
of my rifle with me
I could have shot them both.

Minutes

I do not ask to be winter's tongue:
the ice-spider patiently weaving its thread-thin skim

at the creek edge,
or the long scrape through snow where the beaver

has dragged a fresh cottonwood branch to the river,
or a slush of lights downtown in the village

through an early dark. I ask only
to take the minutes

of the meeting between the season
and myself: the synoptic account

of hoarfrost on the aspen,
and similar motions proposed

by either of us—to be adopted,
postponed, or rejected. In such manner

the slight wheezy call
of an eagle at the top of a snowy hemlock

is transformed along with plough trucks
working by night, boredom,

and the casting of spells into a tally
to be scanned once, perhaps,

then stuffed in a folder or drawer
and likely never exhumed

—except to confirm or find no record of
the pine siskins, the swans overwintering.

Yet I ask because
I am convinced this task

is necessary for democracy,
for the hazel twigs

reddening in February, for the fire
in the cold, and the ice

in the fire. Where there is ice,
one motion reads, water will come once more.

Breath

i

Tufts of snow
that rise from the branch
a chickadee alights on

ii

Winter fog surrounding
the house: on the frosted slope of
the ridge behind, great spruce and pine
blur to white shadows

iii

Straw-coloured humps of grass
interspersed with blotches of snow
are perfectly reflected
on the still surface
of the current

iv

As I ski the river trail
—poles and legs scissoring
like a pendulum—
over me bursts a flight of
tundra swans:
V of white necks, white streamlined bodies

lifting into blue

the mouth of this world
                      exhaling

Afterword: Work and Silence

What is poetry for? Should reading or listening to poetry serve the same function as hearing music does: to provide a mood-creating, -enhancing or -altering experience? Should poetry be an intellectual exercise, an opportunity for readers to sharpen or flaunt their wits by deciphering or guessing at obscurities, allusions, ambiguities, ironies, or omissions in the text? Are there other possible uses for the art?

Those of us who came of age in the 1960s remember when poetry in North America was an influential cultural force, an integral part of the way people, that is to say, society, grappled with the issues of the day: the US struggle for black civil rights (poets Ishmael Reed, Etheridge Knight); opposition to the Vietnam War (Denise Levertov, Robert Bly); feminism (Adrienne Rich, Marge Piercy); and emergent Canadian nationalism (Al Purdy, Dennis Lee). Such *engagé* poetry was featured in newspapers, journals, and other publications devoted to these movements, and was often quoted or recited from behind microphones at rallies, meetings, teach-ins, be-ins. Here in Canada a new book of poems by Irving Layton or Dorothy Livesay or Earle Birney was a public occasion—sparking coverage in the public media, including even television, because the assumption was that poets could speak articulately to the nation at large about matters that affect our collective life.

The longtime US folksinger Pete Seeger in a 2006 *New Yorker* profile mentions that his father—a folklorist—used to state that he was less interested in whether a song was good than in what a song was good *for*. With regard to poetry's function, I agree with the elder Seeger. I have tried to create art that is useful to people engaged in striving for beneficial social change.

I believe my contribution to poetry arises from my poems focused on my work experiences, augmented by my anthologies of, and critical writing about, poems by people depicting the effects on and off the job of their own daily employment. I find the new, insider's, work writing an exciting development in the history of poetry—and by extension, literature: people accurately articulating in poems for the very first time in English what it is like to live a particular job, from cleaning houses to functioning as a corporate executive. Or people broadening and deepening a poetic response to occupations such as logging or the various fields of medicine—jobs concerning which a body of poetry already exists.

I have argued that daily work—how it is organized, and its effects on both individuals and communities—is central to our lives. Work determines or strongly influences where we live, our standard of living, how much time and energy we have during our hours *away* from the job, who our friends are, and a vast range of attitudes to personal and social issues, including the three themes often touted as poetry's preserve: love, nature, and death. No human emotion is absent from the worksite, since a place of employment is where human beings not only gather but where they contribute for good or ill to the daily re-creation of the community.

In my essays I describe why a literature—why an artistic culture—that does not regard and depict work as central to the human story is immature. Children and adolescents are in large part unable to consider work and its import: these young people regard work as at best a peripheral, not a governing concern. My argument is that poetry should not contribute to an infantilization of society.

Where work is not understood to govern human activity, we have the tragedy of nations or peoples who after a bitter struggle to attain a measure of political democracy find that the freedom in daily life that the revolution promised proves to be an illusion: the workplace hierarchies, with their accompanying daily humiliations and oppressions, remain unchanged. Citizens who feel blindsided by their earlier failure to think about economic emancipation often lash out by adopting or supporting political extremism, plunging their society into civil war and/or dictatorship. Also, where work is not understood to be central to human life, a society can declare directly or by implication that people who do no productive work—entertainers of every stripe, for instance, including politicians, actors, athletes who participate in corporatized sporting events—are the community's significant individuals. In contrast, those women and men whose employment results in the provision of food, health, housing, transportation, education, and clothing for the community are regarded as faceless, ignorable, unimportant.

And no resolution of the planetary environmental crisis is possible without first considering how society structures labour. Seahorses could not begin to be saved from extinction until alternative employment was provided for people whose livelihood depended on stripping the ocean of these creatures for sale to pet shop brokers. The Canadian work poet Al Grierson, in his "It's All Our Fault," lists the environmental degradation that is a consequence of the jobs he and his fellow employees have accepted "so our kids could eat oatmeal / and day old bread" and for which "we're ready to take the blame":

> we killed the whales, the seals,
> the buffalo and each other,
> we poisoned the air, polluted the water,

and made this a planet
fit only for insects

we did it for wages;
it's all our fault—
we did it because we didn't know
there was anyone else to go to work for.

The absence in literature up to the present of an accurate insider's account of the experiences and consequences of daily employment echoes the silence in literature for centuries about women's lives. The contemporary women's movement rightly maintains that a literature that ignores or minimizes women's experiences not only implies that such experiences have no value. This literature also cannot claim to be representative of the human story. Since work involves both genders, how much more does the enormous silence around jobs—those anthologies of Canadian poetry, for instance, that present a portrait of a country in which nobody works—give the lie to the claim that our art has value in showing us who we are.

I believe that poetry is ideally suited to break the taboo around a depiction of daily employment. Poetry at the moment is one of the few free spaces in society: that is, poetry is entirely outside the money economy. Even a poet as widely known as the US beat phenomenon Allen Ginsberg made his money by selling his personal papers to a university, not from selling his books of poems. Being outside the money economy gives poets an opportunity to speak the truth without having to give thought to image, branding, polls, the bottom line—considerations that hobble even churches, unions, NGOs, and other ventures supposedly dedicated to speaking about discomfiting or inspirational facets of our common life.

One reason why poetry has shied away from an unblinking look at daily work is that a majority of us are not free on the job. Even in North America, the moment we cross through the office door or the factory gate we enter a sector of society not yet colonized by democracy. During the hours in which we contribute to the community through our labours with body and mind, we are at the beck and call of unelected authorities, who control not only our work processes but also the uses to which the wealth generated by our work are put: how much goes for salaries and bonuses of executives, how much for research and development, how much for maintenance and expansion of physical plant, how much for purchase of raw materials, how much for a return to investors, how much allotted to wages, and so on. We have no say on the impact our job might have on the surrounding biological and human communities.

Afterword / 81

The schizophrenic existence of daily shuttling between the status of an obedient unquestioning employee and that of a critically thinking, free citizen of a democracy—essentially, between being regarded as a child and as an adult—influences our behaviours toward every relationship we have: family, intimate, peer, workmate, community. Navigating the subtleties of this terrain is to me a crucial task for poetry.

Even people aware of the incompatibility of capitalism and democracy, however, often avoid considering the potential of the new work writing in one of two ways. The first is to view contemporary work poetry through the lens of 1930s-style socialist realism. In this approach, work is equated with blue-collar jobs, although very little '30s poetry portrays an accurate insider's view of even blue-collar employment. Socialist realism poetry is instead exhortative, often in vague terms, or deals with instances of social oppression or resistance rather than the details of the workplace and the latter's effect on daily life off the job.

The second route to avoidance of work writing involves focusing on class. This frequently shifts attention from the specifics of a job site to family stories—see, for instance, M.L. Liebler's anthology *Working Words* (Minneapolis: Coffee House Press, 2010). Veering from an unblinking look at employment to considerations of class also means a writer can distance himself or herself from an examination of his or her own work, the lack of freedom found in his or her own daily existence. In academic circles, such gestures toward class often substitute, in my experience, for thinking about work: class is trotted out along with race and gender (and/or sex) as a nontraditional, supposedly fresh way to look at literature. Yet Eric Schocket argues, in *Vanishing Moments: Class and American Literature* (Ann Arbor: University of Michigan Press, 2006), that these alternative critical approaches are far from parallel:

> Whereas race, gender and sexuality can, arguably, name social relationships that are not structured by an unequal distribution of power (this is the dream of pluralism, after all), class—by any definition—can only name a structure, process or position of inequality. John Guillory [in *Cultural Capital: The Problem of Literary Canon Formation* (Chicago: University of Chicago Press, 1993)] writes:
>
>> [W]hile it is easy enough to conceive of a self-affirmative racial or sexual identity, it makes very little sense to posit an affirmative lower-class identity, as such an identity would have to be grounded in the experience of deprivation per se. Acknowledging the existence of admirable and even heroic elements of working-class culture, the *affirmation* of lower-class identity is hardly compatible with a program for the abolition of want.

Schocket goes on to show how discussion of social mobility (a family's ability to escape certain kinds of waged labour) masks the actual conditions of a job that others must endure once certain individuals or their descendants have found different employment.

Despite the vitality and manifold dimensions of the theme of work, I have no illusions about the absence of an audience for art that considers this predominant human experience. Without a vibrant and widespread women's movement, those writers who articulated an accurate insider's account of women's lives found few readers or advocates. Such authors' work was considered marginal, if not forgettable, before a social movement for women's emancipation arose that looked to earlier writers about women's experiences for vindication and inspiration. With the collapse of social change unionism in North America, as a consequence of the Cold War, any interest in emancipation from an economy where work invariably is equated with undemocratic conditions has vanished from the public agenda. Three times in the twentieth century attempts were made to democratize work: the Mahknovist insurrection in Ukraine 1918–1921, the rural and industrial anarchist communities in Aragon and Catalonia in Spain 1936–1939, and the rise of the Solidarity free trade union movement in Poland 1980–1981. But in each instance, the context was civil war, and all three times successes in workplace self-management were decisively overturned by the armed forces of reaction. Without a North American broad social movement that embraces the extension of democracy to the workplace, the audience for the new work writing will remain tiny.

In the academy, where some sustained interest in poetry remains, much of the thinking about literature is driven by the needs of graduate students, who must find an original topic in order to produce a thesis. As apprentices, graduate students must continually defer to authority: ideas must be defended by reference to certain approved critics, thesis supervisors must be obeyed or mollified, and go-through the-motions conference papers must be presented to bulk up resumés in the hope of eventually landing a job, acquiring graduate students of one's own, and repeating the authoritarian cycle. This pattern hardly trains women and men capable of thinking about the democratization of employment. Ironically, however, activist faculty unionism has led in at least one jurisdiction to the ending of the practice followed by so many universities of stringing along new or prospective faculty for decades with a series of temporary contracts (sessional work). In the B.C. community college system, two hard-fought faculty strikes won the regularization first of positions, then individuals, to successfully halt the increasing use of sessionals by college administrations (in imitation of their university administration colleagues). Yet in other jurisdictions, Alberta for example, post-secondary faculty accept

Afterword / 83

that by legislation they are forbidden to function as members of a normal trade union (i.e., strikes are illegal), with consequences such as faculty collective agreements (the University of Calgary's, for instance) that do not specify conditions of employment, meaning that some departments have a heavier teaching load than others for the same remuneration.

Whatever the lack of a contemporary audience for work poetry, however, the potential for a wider readership has influenced my choices with regard to poetic form. In an essay I wrote about quotidian poets for Volume II of David Carpenter's *The Literary History of Saskatchewan* (Regina: Coteau, 2014) I describe these poets' compositional strategies, strategies that my own writing has largely adopted:

> Where a poet's role is seen as contributing to a community's self-awareness, and hence self-confidence (including an accompanying belief in the right to self-govern), the task of the writer is to speak of and to his or her community: to observe and record how the members of the community cope with their individual, and common, economic, social and political lives. The poet is not viewed as a possessor of special, esoteric (frequently jargonized) wisdom about either social organization or language. Therefore direct plain speech is the operative mode for poetry: the poet adopts free verse, a conversational tone and diction, and stanzas and line indents employed like paragraphs to indicate shifts in thought, mood or subject. Where a poet regards herself or himself as a member of the community described, ironic distance is eschewed, and the poet's attention to her or his own reactions to objects, events, individuals, others' emotions, etc., is held to be one more example of how we as a people are coping with the economic, social, political and personal vagaries of our existences.
>
> In order for the poet to communicate clearly his or her own strong *emotional* responses to objects, events and individuals, or the responses of fellow community members, the poet will embrace the lyric mode. To *detail* the significant moments that illustrate the historical or geographical situation, the poet adopts the narrative or anecdotal mode. Because community exists in a specific time and place, in poetry the quotidian is emphasized over abstruse philosophy. Wisdom is regarded as located in our reflected-upon personal experiences or those of our fellow citizens as much or more as it is found in the thinking of Great Men or Women.

That said, I view my poems as scores for oral delivery. No poem of mine is considered finished unless I decide it is effective when spoken aloud as well as when read silently. This attention to how the poem sounds influences my choices of diction, pacing, grammatical construction, and much more.

And of course my poems encompass a wider spectrum than the workplace. My first collection was published in 1973, so over forty years and more I have responded to natural and constructed environments, the vicissitudes of love, the pleasures of the road. And, in the long tradition, *timor mortis conturbat me*. I have tried in my poems whatever their topic to deploy precision of observation, humour, and honesty to help convey what I mean to say. But I do not feel my poems on other themes rototill new poetic ground in the way my poems do that arise from the work experience—except where I have been able to insinuate into the former type of poem an awareness of the labour that, acknowledged or not, infuses the world.

—*Tom Wayman*

Acknowledgements

Owen Percy:
Thanks first and foremost to Tom Wayman for his poems, and for his patience, optimism, hospitality, guidance, and friendship. Thanks also to WLUP for their hard work and their dedication to poetry in this country. A debt of gratitude is also owed to Howard White, Billy Collins, and Fred Wah for their generosity and enthusiasm. This volume would not have come to fruition without the love and guidance of Robyn Read.

Tom Wayman:
My thanks to the staffs of the publishers who for more than forty years have been hospitable to my poems. I am especially grateful to Howard White of Harbour Publishing. His consistent generosity toward my words over the decades has been a source of both encouragement and inspiration.

    Thanks as well to Owen Percy for conceiving of this project. I believe the future of Canadian literary studies is in good hands as long as the profession can attract young scholars who like Owen combine practicality, intellect, and a deep-rooted love of imaginative writing.

From *Waiting for Wayman* (Toronto: McClelland & Stewart, 1973)
    Days: Construction
    Picketing Supermarkets
    Wayman in Love

From *For and Against the Moon: Blues, Yells, and Chuckles* (Toronto: Macmillan, 1974)
    The Country of Everyday: Literary Criticism

From *Money and Rain: Tom Wayman Live!* (Toronto: Macmillan, 1975)
    The Factory Hour
    The Old Power

From *Free Time: Industrial Poems* (Toronto: Macmillan, 1977)
    Industrial Music
    Factory Time

From *Living on the Ground: Tom Wayman Country* (Toronto: McClelland & Stewart, 1980)
    Garrison
    Friday Night in Early September at Morris and Sara Wayman's Farm, Roseneath, Ontario

From *Counting the Hours: City Poems* (Toronto: McClelland & Stewart, 1983)
    White Hand

From *The Face of Jack Munro* (Madeira Park, BC: Harbour, 1986)
    Silos
    Paper, Scissors, Stone
    The Face of Jack Munro

From *In a Small House on the Outskirts of Heaven* (Madeira Park, BC: Harbour, 1989)
    A Cursing Poem: This Poem Wants Gordon Shrum to Die
    The Poet
    Defective Parts of Speech: Official Errata

From *Did I Miss Anything? Selected Poems, 1973–1993* (Madeira Park, BC: Harbour, 1993)
    Did I Miss Anything?

From *The Astonishing Weight of the Dead* (Vancouver: Polestar, 1994)
    The Man Who Logged the West Ridge

From *I'll Be Right Back: New and Selected Poems, 1980–1996* (Princeton, NJ: Ontario Review Press, 1997.)
    For William Stafford (1914–1993)

From *The Colours of the Forest* (Madeira Park, BC: Harbour, 1999)
    War on a Round Planet

From *My Father's Cup* (Madeira Park, BC: Harbour, 2002)
    Cup
    Epithalamium for a Former Lover

From *High Speed Through Shoaling Water* (Madeira Park, BC: Harbour, 2007)
  Calgary
  Postmodern 911

From *Dirty Snow* (Madeira Park, BC: Harbour, 2012)
  Mt. Gimli Pashtun
  Air Support
  Whistle

From *Winter's Skin* (Fernie, BC: Oolichan, 2013)
  The White Dogs
  Minutes
  Breath

lps Books in the Laurier Poetry Series
Published by Wilfrid Laurier University Press

derek beaulieu   *Please, No More Poetry: The Poetry of derek beaulieu*, edited by Kit Dobson, with an afterword by Lori Emerson • 2013 • xvi + 74 pp. • ISBN 978-1-55458-829-9

Dionne Brand   *Fierce Departures: The Poetry of Dionne Brand*, edited by Leslie C. Sanders, with an afterword by Dionne Brand • 2009 • xvi + 44 pp. • ISBN 978-1-55458-038-5

Di Brandt   *Speaking of Power: The Poetry of Di Brandt*, edited by Tanis MacDonald, with an afterword by Di Brandt • 2006 • xvi + 56 pp. • ISBN-10: 0-88920-506-X; ISBN-13: 978-0-88920-506-2

Nicole Brossard   *Mobility of Light: The Poetry of Nicole Brossard*, edited by Louise H. Forsyth, with an afterword by Nicole Brossard • 2009 • xxvi + 118 pp. • ISBN 978-1-55458-047-7

George Elliott Clarke   *Blues and Bliss: The Poetry of George Elliott Clarke*, edited by Jon Paul Fiorentino, with an afterword by George Elliott Clarke • 2008 • xviii + 72 pp. • ISBN 978-1-55458-060-6

Dennis Cooley   *By Word of Mouth: The Poetry of Dennis Cooley*, edited by Nicole Markotić, with an afterword by Dennis Cooley • 2007 • xxii + 62 pp. • ISBN-10: 1-55458-007-2; ISBN-13: 978-1-55458-007-1

Lorna Crozier   *Before the First Word: The Poetry of Lorna Crozier*, edited by Catherine Hunter, with an afterword by Lorna Crozier • 2005 • xviii + 62 pp. • ISBN-10: 0-88920-489-6; ISBN-13: 978-0-88920-489-8

Christopher Dewdney   *Children of the Outer Dark: The Poetry of Christopher Dewdney*, edited by Karl E. Jirgens, with an afterword by Christopher Dewdney • 2007 • xviii + 60 pp. • ISBN-10: 0-88920-515-9; ISBN-13: 978-0-88920-515-4

Don Domanski   *Earthly Pages: The Poetry of Don Domanski*, edited by Brian Bartlett, with an afterword by Don Domanski • 2007 • xvi + 62 pp. • ISBN-10: 1-55458-008-0; ISBN-13: 978-1-55458-008-8

Louis Dudek   *All These Roads: The Poetry of Louis Dudek*, edited by Karis Shearer, with an afterword by Frank Davey • 2008 • xx + 70 pp. • ISBN 978-1-55458-039-2

George Fetherling   *Plans Deranged by Time: The Poetry of George Fetherling*, edited by A.F. Moritz, with an afterword by George Fetherling • 2012 • xviii + 64 pp. • ISBN 978-1-55458-631-8

M. Travis Lane   *The Crisp Day Closing on My Hand: The Poetry of M. Travis Lane*, edited by Jeanette Lynes, with an afterword by M. Travis Lane • 2007 • xvi + 86 pp. • ISBN-10: 1-55458-025-0; ISBN-13: 978-1-55458-025-5

Tim Lilburn   *Desire Never Leaves: The Poetry of Tim Lilburn*, edited by Alison Calder, with an afterword by Tim Lilburn • 2007 • xiv + 50 pp. • ISBN-10: 0-88920-514-0; ISBN-13: 978-0-88920-514-7

Eli Mandel   *From Room to Room: The Poetry of Eli Mandel*, edited by Peter Webb, with an afterword by Andrew Stubbs • 2011 • xviii + 66 pp. • ISBN 978-1-55458-255-6

Steve McCaffery   *Verse and Worse: Selected and New Poems of Steve McCaffery 1989–2009*, edited by Darren Wershler, with an afterword by Steve McCaffery • 2010 • xiv + 76 pp. • ISBN 978-1-55458-188-7

Don McKay   *Field Marks: The Poetry of Don McKay*, edited by Méira Cook, with an afterword by Don McKay • 2006 • xxvi + 60 pp. • ISBN-10: 0-88920-494-2; ISBN-13: 978-0-88920-494-2

Al Purdy   *The More Easily Kept Illusions: The Poetry of Al Purdy*, edited by Robert Budde, with an afterword by Russell Brown • 2006 • xvi + 80 pp. • ISBN-10: 0-88920-490-X; ISBN-13: 978-0-88920-490-4

F.R. Scott   *Leaving the Shade of the Middle Ground: The Poetry of F.R. Scott*, edited by Laura Moss, with an afterword by George Elliott Clarke • 2011 • xxiv + 72 pp. • ISBN 978-1-55458-367-6

Fred Wah   *The False Laws of Narrative: The Poetry of Fred Wah*, edited by Louis Cabri, with an afterword by Fred Wah • 2009 • xxiv + 78 pp. • ISBN 978-1-555458-046-0

Tom Wayman   *The Order in Which We Do Things: The Poetry of Tom Wayman*, edited by Owen Percy, with an afterword by Tom Wayman • 2014 • xx + 92 pp. • ISBN 978-1-55458-995-1

www.ingramcontent.com/pod-product-compliance
Lightning Source LLC
Chambersburg PA
CBHW071214070526
44584CB00019B/3031